Seven Taoist Masters

SEVEN TAOIST MASTERS

A Folk Novel of China

Translated by Eva Wong

SHAMBHALA
Boston & London
1990

Shambhala Publications, Inc.
Horticultural Hall
300 Massachusetts Avenue
Boston, Massachusetts 02115
www.shambhala.com

17   16   15   14   13   12
Printed in the United States of America
⊗ This edition is printed on acid-free paper that meets the
American National Standards Institute Z39.48 Standard.
Distributed in the United States by Random House, Inc.,
and in Canada by Random House of Canada Ltd

Library of Congress Cataloging-in-Publication Data
Seven Taoist masters : a folk novel of China / translated by
Eva Wong.—1st ed.
p.   cm.
ISBN 0-87773-544-1 (alk. paper)
1. Spiritual life (Taoism)   I. Wong, Eva, 1951–
BL1923.S44   1990
299′.5144—dc20   89-43307
CIP

To my respected teacher, Mr. Moy Lin-shin,
who showed me the path of
the return to the origin

Contents

Illustrations

Acknowledgments

I would first like to thank my teacher, Master Moy Lin-shin, for giving me the teachings of the Tao. Through him I have learned to live a more meaningful life. I owe him my health and my wellness of being, and, most important of all, through his example I have learned compassion and selflessless.

Also, many thanks to my friend and fellow temple member Karen Laughlin for reading through the early version of the manuscript and making valuable comments and suggestions.

Finally, thanks to the many members of Fung Loy Kok Taoist Temple and the Taoist Tai Chi Society who have supported the temple's Translation Committee. Without their encouragement, this work would not have been possible.

Translator's Introduction

In the spring of 1981 I met a man who would change the course of my life forever. His name is Moy Lin-shin; he is a Taoist monk who emigrated to Canada from Hong Kong. It was through him that I was initiated into a Taoist temple and received the teachings of the Tao.

As a child growing up in Hong Kong, I was fascinated by stories of Taoist masters and immortals. When I began my study of the Chinese classics at age fourteen, I was strangely drawn to the Taoist philosophy of Chuang-tzu and Huai-nan-tzu and had no interest in the romantic poetry and novels that were popular with youngsters my age. Throughout my adolescent years, while I studied the *I Ching* and the geomantic art of *feng-shui* with my granduncle, I also gained some knowledge of the more obscure texts of the Taoist canon. But I was told that if I wanted to pursue Taoist training seriously, I needed to find a Taoist master. When I finished high school in Hong Kong, my parents decided that I should pursue a college education in the United States. During my university years in Boston and New York City, I tried to find a Taoist teacher but failed. Then, through a number of unexpected circumstances, I moved to Buffalo and met Moy Lin-shin at a meditation workshop at a local *t'ai-chi* club. In my first encounter with him I knew intuitively that this man would be my teacher, and that I would entrust to him my spiritual growth and development. The mutual acceptance and trust that formed the bond of a master-disciple relationship was forged, and before he left he encouraged me to visit him in Toronto as often as I could. Within a year of our meeting I was initiated into the Taoist temple he had cofounded, and soon after that I was allowed to address him as "Sifu" (Respected Teacher). In 1987, I began to travel with my Sifu in North America, Europe, and Australia, acting as an assistant and interpreter at his *t'ai-chi* and *ch'i-kung* workshops. Then in the summer of 1988, while I was assisting him at a one-week seminar on Taoism, he said to me, "You must translate the book called *Seven Taoist Masters*, for it is one of the best introductions to the teachings of Taoism." At the conclusion of the seminar I returned to my home in Colorado and began working on the translation.

Seven Taoist Masters is a manual of Taoist training written in the form of a popular novel. The Taoist sages know that the best way to teach the philosophy and principles of training in Taoism is to present the material in a way that captures the interest of the reader. Storytelling had been used very effectively in China to convey Buddhist and Taoist teachings. As the novel emerged during the Ming dynasty (1368–1644) as a form of literary expression, it became an ideal vehicle for introducing abstract and often esoteric teachings of Taoism and Buddhism to the general populace. Moreover, since novels were written in the vernacular rather than in classical Chinese, knowledge that had previously been available only to the scholar-aristocracy was now open to the less educated. As a result, books such as *Journey to the West, Heroes of the Marsh, Seven Taoist Masters*, and *Romance of the Three Kingdoms* enjoyed tremendous popularity with the Chinese people and became household tales that every Chinese child grew up with.

The authorship of *Seven Taoist Masters* is unknown. The literary style suggests that it was written during the middle part of the Ming dynasty (circa 1500). The novel developed from storytelling, which itself can be traced back to the saga-songs of Mongol (Yüan) culture. The sympathetic attitude toward the Yüan emperor in the novel also suggests that the text was written during a time when the memory of the atrocities of the Mongol emperors had faded.

Many Taoist stories trace a history of oral transmission before their appearance in written form. Unlike the tales of the *Lieh Tzu*, which were transmitted orally for several hundred years before they were collected in written form, *Seven Taoist Masters* probably originated in storytelling but was written and published shortly after it attained popularity. Its literary style differs from that of "true novels" like *Journey to the West* and *Heroes of the Marsh* in that it contains phrases reminiscent of mnemonics used by blind storytellers.

In *Seven Taoist Masters*, the experiences of Wang Ch'ung-yang and his seven disciples describe the appropriate personal attitude and environmental settings needed for Taoist training, as well as the obstacles typically encountered on the path to enlightenment. Wang Ch'ung-yang and his disciples were historical figures who lived in the eras of the Southern Sung (1127–1279) and Yüan (1271–1368) dynasties. History records that the disciple Ch'iu Ch'ang-ch'un was befriended by Kublai Khan and was appointed court high priest during the reign of the first Yüan emperor, T'ai Tzu. His successors continued to be favored by Chinese emperors through the Ming and Ching (1645–1911) dynasties. *Seven Taoist Masters* weaves history and legend together to tell a tale that entertains as it instructs.

Wang Ch'ung-yang is regarded as one of the greatest patriarchs of the School of True Reality (or the School of Complete Reality). His students, the Seven Taoist Masters, are considered to be the holders of the transmission of the Northern School of Taoism, the branch of Taoism that advocates the "singular path." In "singular-path" Taoism, enlightenment (and immortality) are achieved through meditation and *ch'i-kung* exercises rather than through sexual yoga or the ingestion of herbs. Immortality is attained through internal alchemy, that is, the transformation of mind and body through the efforts of the individual. In fact, Ch'iu Ch'ang-ch'un, one of the seven masters, went on to found the Lung-men ("Dragon Gate") sect of Taoism. Since then, the Lung-men sect has remained one of the most prominent of the "singular-path" Taoist sects.

Seven Taoist Masters introduces Taoist teachings directly in the form of "lectures" given by Wang Ch'ung-yang, the teacher of the seven masters, and indirectly in the description of the experiences of the seven masters in their pursuit of enlightenment. The lectures of Wang Ch'ung-yang, Ch'iu Ch'ang-ch'un, and other characters paraphrase and explain the more abstract and esoteric texts of the Taoist canon concerning the nature of mind and body, the levels of Taoist training, meditation techniques, and how to overcome the four great obstacles to Taoist training: drunkenness, sexual desire, wealth, and anger.

The indirect method of conveying Taoist wisdom, which is embodied in the story's action, is probably the more powerful vehicle of teaching. Events in stories linger long after the reader has closed the book, entering the nonconscious mind with less resistance than explicit assertions of principles. In general, Taoist teachings are more accessible in an intuitive reading than in an analytic reading of a text. As we "lose" ourselves in the story, our ego becomes less active in discrimination and analysis. And when the ego loses its grip on consciousness, the mind can become more receptive to the wisdom that is presented to us.

The experiences of the seven masters describe the personal attitude required for cultivating the Tao, the physical and social environments conducive to Taoist training, and the obstacles that lie on the path to enlightenment.

Taoist names allude to the principles of theory and practice in Taoist training. The names of Wang Ch'ung-yang and his seven disciples all point to various aspects of Taoist internal alchemy. Below is a list of the names and their translation.

Wang Ch'ung-yang

Ch'ung-yang translates as "the rebirth of *yang*." "*Yang*" is taken here to mean "life" and "growth." Together, the name means a rejuvenation of mind and body.

Ma Tan-yang

Tan-yang translates as "the bright, pure pill." The "pill" is the Golden Pill, the result of the synthesis of the three internal energies (generative, vital, and spiritual energy) in their pure form. "Bright" and "pure" are qualities associated with the Golden Pill. Together, the name refers to the emergence of the Golden Pill. The emergence of the Pill is the prerequisite for the conception and development of the spirit, the vehicle that transports the individual into the immortal plane.

Sun Pu-erh

Pu-erh translates as "no second way." The "second way" refers to paths that stray from the Tao. Acknowledging that there is no "second way" means that one has made the resolution to pursue the Tao with singleness of mind.

Ch'iu Ch'ang-ch'un

Ch'ang-ch'un translates as "eternal spring." "Eternal spring" refers to a state of continuous growth. A being whose body is like eternal spring is an immortal.

Liu Ch'ang-sheng

Ch'ang-sheng translates as "longevity" or "eternal life." For centuries in China, Taoism was referred to as the "art of the cultivation of longevity."

T'an Ch'ang-chen

Ch'ang-chen translates as "forever enlightened" or "eternal enlightenment." A Taoist sage is often referred to as one whose enlightenment is real and lasting.

Hao T'ai-ku

T'ai-ku translates as "the ancient." The Huang-lao philosophy, which emerged in the Han dynasties (206 B.C.E.–219 C.E.) regarded Lao-tzu and the Yellow Emperor (Huang-ti) as cofounders of Taoism. The era of the Yellow Emperor was seen as a period in which the teachings of the Tao were practiced, by ruler and people. This legendary period of prehistoric China came to be known as "the ancient days," and the teachings of the Yellow Emperor "the ancient ways." Reference to "Ancient" within Taoism implies following the way of the Yellow Emperor and Lao-tzu.

Wang Yü-yang

Yü-yang translates as "bright jade." In Taoist symbolism, the enlightened consciousness is often described as a piece of pure jade. In Taoist religion, the most enlightened beings dwell in a realm called the Palace of Pure Jade. Its overseer is the Heavenly Lord of Wu-chi, who presided over existence when things were still in the undifferentiated state. Beings who manage to attain this level of enlightenment are said to have merged with the Tao in its original undifferentiated state.

The seven disciples—Ma Tan-yang, Sun Pu-erh, Ch'iu Ch'ang-ch'un, Liu Ch'ang-sheng, T'an Ch'ang-chen, Hao T'ai-ku, and Wang Yü-yang—represent different approaches to the Tao. Ma Tan-Yang comes to enlightenment through simplicity in thought and action. Sun Pu-erh takes the most difficult path—the total abandonment of the ego through sheer discipline of mind and body. Ch'iu Ch'ang-ch'un keeps to his path through unshakable faith in the teachings of the Tao in the face of hardships. Liu Ch'ang-sheng's flight of intuition leads him to experience directly the mysterious ways of the Tao by using desire to counter desire. T'an Ch'ang-chen sticks to his quest through incredible stability of mind and discipline. Hao T'ai-ku attains the Tao through selfless giving. Wang Yü-yang finds the Tao through absolute stillness in meditation.

Each of the seven disciples also has to surmount an obstacle that constitutes the most intransigent part of his or her ego. For Ma Tan-yang, it is complacency. He needs his wife, Sun Pu-erh, to decide for him what he should do. When the other disciples accompany Wang Ch'ung-yang on his travels, Ma Tan-yang stays behind. When the group of disciples disbands after Wang Ch'ung-yang's departure to the immortal realm, Ma Tan-yang falls into laziness and does not train as rigorously as the others. It is only when Sun Pu-erh returns briefly to check his progress that Ma Tan-yang finally realizes that complacency is preventing him from advancing. For Sun Pu-erh, the obstacle is intellectualism. She studies the Taoist scriptures before being initiated into Taoist training by Wang Ch'ung-yang. Much of her doubt and her inability to transcend written knowledge with practical training is founded on her assumptions of what Taoist training is all about. For Ch'iu Ch'ang-ch'un the obstacle is impatience. Ch'iu Ch'ang-ch'un cannot restrain himself from interrupting Wang Ch'ung-yang's lactures and voicing his opinions in front of others. He wants to learn things that are far beyond his capacity. Even when he has made much progress in his training he jumps to conclusions prematurely and would have taken his own life if the

Lords of Heaven had not intervened to save him. For Liu Ch'ang-sheng, it is sexual desire. He fantasizes being invited to a gathering at the Palace of the Empress of Heaven. Unable to control his desire, he glances at the Empress's court ladies out of the corner of his eye. T'an Ch'ang-chen's obstacle is pride. Pride makes him sit outside the Ku family mansion until he is admitted inside. Even then, when he is acknowledged as a "teacher of Tao," pride makes him stay at the Ku mansion until he realizes that for the good of his student and for himself he should leave. For Hao T'ai-ku, it is rigidity. Sitting under the bridge by the river, Hao T'ai-ku forms an impression that Taoist meditation means "quiet sitting" and does not abandon his self-imposed vigil until a Taoist immortal shows him alternatives. For Wang Yü-yang, it is his competitive attitude. In order to win his duel with an imposter, he turns the practice of Taoist meditation into a competition and forces himself to sit for an unnatural length of time.

Seven Taoist Masters is also about the personal sacrifices that one needs to make in order to complete Taoist training. Wang Ch'ung-yang sacrifices his wealth and social position in his village by pretending to be stricken with an incurable disease. Ma Tan-yang generously gives his wealth to Wang Ch'ung-yang for building a Taoist retreat and supporting a community of Taoist recluses. Sun Pu-erh sacrifices her beauty and intellectualism by immolating her face and becoming a beggar to live among the lowest social class. Ch'iu Ch'ang-ch'un's sacrifice is probably the greatest. He repeatedly sacrifices comfort and material gain. He is even willing to give up his life so that the life of another can be saved. Liu Ch'ang-sheng is able to ignore the comments of others who taunt him for his sojourns at the brothels. In this way, he sacrifices external respect to achieve internal development. T'an Ch'ang-chen gives up the life of comfort provided for him by his student to return to the life of a begging monk. Without a second thought Hao T'ai-ku relinquishes the meditation caves that he had excavated for himself to other Taoist hermits. Wang Yü-yang gives up an opportunity to be a respected Taoist teacher so that he may continue his training in peace. There are many other incidents in which personal sacrifice is called for, and none of the seven masters hesitates to give up what is demanded of them. Taoist training is no easy matter. Although described in prototypical form, the tremendous efforts and personal sacrifices required for attaining immortality described in the book are not exaggerated.

Apart from personal conviction and discipline, environmental conditions and support from family and friends are also crucial in Taoist training. Sun Pu-erh is told to go to a place of spiritual power and live in isolation to facilitate her training. Wang Ch'ung-yang builds a retreat in Ma Tan-yang's mansion complete with meditation rooms and a lecture hall so that people with similar spiritual interests can mutually support each other. T'an Ch'ang-chen leaves the Ku mansion because too much comfort can retard spiritual training. Hao T'ai-ku achieves enlightenment in the isolated cliff-caves of Hua-shan. For Liu Ch'ang-sheng, the brothels provide an environment in which he can confront his sexual desires and dissolve them. Ch'iu Ch'ang-ch'un lives in extreme conditions, from abandoned temples to remote river gorges, so that he can temper his nature and tame his heart.

In *Seven Taoist Masters* we also see that support from family and friends is important in Taoist training. First, witness the total lack of support from Wang Ch'ung-yang's wife and friends. As a result he has to feign ill health and madness before he can practice Taoism in peace. This constitutes the most unsupportive family environment. Next, consider the "noninterfering" attitude of Ch'iu Ch'ang-ch'un's brothers. They let him pursue his interests in peace, but they do not provide active support and encouragement. This lack of active support is hinted at in Ch'iu Ch'ang-ch'un's secret departure from his home. The family environment is not hostile, but if there is any support, it is passive rather than active. The relationship between Ma Tan-yang and Sun Pu-erh represents the ideal environmental condition for Taoist training. Husband and wife have the same interests, and both are willing to sacrifice their physical relationship for spiritual advancement. Chao Pi and his friends are able to give up a life of living outside the law and finally become Taoist monks because, as a closely-knit circle of friends, they are able to provide one another with the moral support needed to change their lives.

Throughout the book numerous incidents illustrate the Taoist belief that karma is built from actions. Reward and retribution will be given according to one's actions. Destiny can be changed by human actions, and the foundations necessary to Taoist training may have been laid in previous lifetimes.

Seven Taoist Masters is a book about correct thought and action in Taoist living. In Taoism, the development of the body is intricately tied to the taming of the mind. This is especially so at the more advanced levels of Taoist training. My master, Moy Lin-shin, has gradually given me more advice on taming the desires and egoistic tendencies of the mind while conducting my daily life, rather than specific instructions in meditation, *ch'i-kung,* and the internal martial arts. A mind tamed of attachment facilitates the body's response to the methods of cultivating and circulating internal energy. As a matter of fact, the practice of Taoist *ch'i-kung* is extremely dangerous if the ego is dominant. The taming of the mind is accomplished and reflected in our daily life.

In *Seven Taoist Masters* we are presented with the examples of seven remarkable individuals who not only mastered the theory of Taoism and internal alchemy but lived it. As a part of the Taoist canon, it is considered by major Taoist sects as an introduction to Taoism for both the novice initiate and the lay public. It may be read as a manual of Taoist training, but then again it may simply be read as a story of seven individuals who overcome tremendous hardships on a path to self-discovery and fulfillment.

Seven Taoist Masters

$Charitable\ deeds$ are not meant to be a public perfor-
mance. If you display compassion in order to show others your
virtue, then your actions are empty of meaning. No matter how
much you give to the poor, if you are doing it only to impress
others, it is not charity.

During the Sung dynasty (960–1279 C.E.) in Shensi Province
there was a small village of some 100 residents, called Ta-wei.
Most of the villagers belonged to the Wang clan. In this clan was
a widow about forty years old. She had a son and daughter but
now both had married and left home. This woman had a kindly
and maternal nature and would treat all the children in the village
as her own. She gave them food and gifts, and would comfort
them if they were hurt. All the children knew that if they needed
help they could call on her. Her kindness was so well known that
the villagers called her Mother Wang. Mother Wang was also
quite wealthy and deeply religious. She invited Buddhist and
Taoist monks to her home for vegetarian dinners, gave sizable
donations to the monasteries, and chanted the sutras regularly.
Even beggars and orphans from neighboring villages would come
to her for help.

One winter it was unusually cold. Snow fell in thick drifts on
the ground, and the wind blew hard. The streets were deserted;
the entire village seemed desolate. One cold, dark evening two
beggars arrived at the home of Mother Wang, asking for food and
shelter. When Mother Wang saw them she said, "You are young
and strong. Why are you begging? Why can't you find an honest
trade instead of living off the charity of others? If you expect
help from me, you must be out of your minds!"

Scarcely had she finished talking to the beggars when a Buddhist and a Taoist monk arrived, asking for rice and vegetables.
Immediately Mother Wang sent a servant to fill the begging
bowls of the monks with food. When the monks had left, the
two beggars asked Mother Wang, "Kind lady, why is it that you

gave food to the monks and not to us?" Mother Wang replied, "I gladly attend to the needs of monks, because although I give them a bowl of rice and vegetables, in return they give me more. The Buddhist monk can chant for me so that no disasters befall me. The Taoist monk can teach me methods of prolonging life. But you? What can I get in return for helping you?" The beggars said, "If your compassion and charity are sincere, you will give without expecting anything in return. If you expect to get something out of what you give, then it is not true charity. All this time your charitable deeds have been either a show for others to see or an investment in the hope of obtaining long life and prosperity." After saying these words the beggars left.

By now night had fallen and the snow was falling more heavily. The two beggars reached the outskirts of the village, where dwellings were sparse. They came to a house with a large black door and called loudly to the master of the house. After a while, footsteps were heard and the door opened. The beggars found themselves standing in front of a tall, bearded man about forty years old. Although middle-aged, the man was of strong physique and appeared to have the bearing of one well-trained in the martial arts. This man was named Wang T'ieh-hsin. In his youth he had studied the classics and had aspired to become a government official. However, he had repeatedly failed the civil service examinations and became disillusioned with scholarly pursuits. Subsequently he abandoned the study of the classics and trained himself in the martial arts, becoming a knight who championed the cause of the poor and oppressed. On this winter night, he and his wife, son, and servants were roasting meat in front of the fire when the beggars knocked on his door.

Wang T'ieh-hsin saw the two beggars standing in the snow with thin clothing and bare feet. Immediately he said, "The night is cold, and you are at the edge of the village. You will not find another house nearby. No one should be traveling in this storm, let alone you who have no shoes and no winter coats. Why don't you come in with me? I have a guest room where you can spend the night and wait until the storm is over before you continue your way." The beggars were delighted and thanked

憐貧困偶施小惠
入夢寐深指迷途

于栖

The two beggars arrive at the door of Master Wang's mansion.
Master Wang dreams of his visit to the Lake of Lotus with the
two beggars.

Wang many times. Wang led them to the guest room and ordered his servants to bring in warm blankets and a hot meal.

The beggars stayed at Wang's home for two days while the storm raged outside. On the third day the snow stopped and the weather warmed. The two beggars decided it was time to leave, but as they were leaving their room they saw Wang approaching them, followed by a servant bearing a tray of food and wine. "I have been busy taking care of some business the last two days and did not give you the hospitality that you as guests should receive. Today I would like to eat and drink and talk freely with you." The beggars accepted his invitation gladly, and the three of them drank and ate and talked like old friends. When much had been said and much drunk, Wang asked his two guests, "Why are you beggars? Is it because you lost your money? Or were you cheated by unscrupulous people? What skills do you have? Maybe I can help you restart your business by giving you some money." One of the beggars replied, "My name is Gold-Is-Heavy. His," pointing to his friend, "is Empty-Mind Ch'ang. We have been beggars all our lives. Even if you gave us money we would not know how to run a business. We are used to living without the weight of gold. When there is food, we eat. When we are tired, we find a place to sleep. We would rather be like the wild geese flying free than like the domestic hen that never frees itself from material needs. If you aspire to fame and fortune, how can you free your spirit from the earthly realm?"

When Wang heard these words he sighed and said, "You are both sages who have freed yourselves from the material clutches of this eartlhy existence. I respect your wishes and will not press you any more. But I envy you, for you are not attached to the world."

The next day, Wang saw the two beggars off and accompanied them to the edge of the village. They said goodbye, but Wang was loath to return home, and kept on walking with them. After a while they came to a bridge. The beggars stepped onto it and beckoned Wang to follow. Wang stared at the bridge. For as long as he had lived in that area, he had never seen a bridge at the edge of the village. He hesitated, but his friends were calling

4

him to follow them. He could hear them saying, "Riches and fortune will disappear. Even the best clothes will wear out and become rags. The two of us have left the material world. We do not owe anybody anything, and we do not care about success and failure. What we have robbers cannot take away. The sun and moon are our companions. We do not bow down to anyone. We are poor, and yet we possess the greatest treasure of all."

When Wang heard these words he hesitated no longer. He stepped onto the bridge and crossed over to the other side of the river. There he found the two beggars sitting at a table with food and wine. After drinking a few cups Wang felt lightheaded and sleepy. His two friends invited him to join them on a trip to a beautiful lake on top of a mountain. Wang had no sense of how long and how far they traveled. When they arrived at the foot of a high mountain, Empty-Mind Ch'ang began to climb up the steep slopes. Wang looked at the cliffs and wondered if he would be able to climb them. Reading his mind, Gold-Is-Heavy said, "Don't be afraid. Just follow my steps. You'll find that you can climb effortlessly." Wang did what he was told, and at once his body became weightless and he seemed to float up the side of the mountain. When he reached the top, Wang saw a lake of clear, tranquil water. In the middle of the lake were seven golden lotus flowers in full bloom. Wang looked at the flowers, and as if he could read Wang's thoughts, Empty-Mind Ch'ang said, "They are beautiful, aren't they? Do you wish that you could have them?" Before Wang could reply, Empty-Mind Ch'ang had walked across the water and returned to his side with the lotus flowers in his hand. He handed the flowers to Wang and said, "Take care of these flowers. They are the spirits of seven enlight-ened souls destined to be your disciples. Their karma is tied to yours. When you meet them, remember Gold-Is-Heavy and Empty-Mind Ch'ang and the seven flowers we have entrusted to your care." Wang carefully put the flowers in his robe. "Is there a chance that we will meet again?" Wang asked the two friends. Empty-Mind Ch'ang said, "We should meet again before too long, perhaps three months from now. Look for me by the bridge where our karmas are intertwined."

Wang bid farewell to his friends and started down the mountain. Suddenly his foot tripped over some undergrowth and he fell. Unable to stop his fall, he rolled over a cliff and totally lost consciousness.

2

When Wang came to his senses he found himself lying on a couch in his study. "That was a long dream," he thought. As he slowly opened his eyes he saw his son standing beside him. Now he remembered everything. It was not a dream. The boy cried, "Father is awake!" Wang's wife hurried into the study to tend to him, and asked him if he was all right. Wang murmured, "Strange indeed. I remembered that I saw the beggars off and walked to the edge of the village with them. How did I come to be lying on a bed in my study?" His wife replied, "You left with the two beggars yesterday. When evening came and we did not see you, I sent some servants to look for you. They found you some twenty miles from our village, sleeping next to a bridge. They tried to wake you up, but you appeared drunk and asleep, so they carried you home. You have slept for a night and a day and have woken only now." She then gently reprimanded him, saying, "Husband, you have earned yourself fame and respect in this area. You are known to everyone as a virtuous man. If people find you in the company of beggars or drunk by the roadside, you will lose your reputation. Many look up to you. You are an example to the young men. In the future you must pay attention to what you do and the company you keep." Wang thanked his wife for her advice and said, "Woman, I think the two beggars are no ordinary people but immortals visiting the earthly realm." His wife said, "Immortals do not dress themselves in rags. Clearly those two were only beggars." But Wang explained, "From the way they talked and how they behaved, I am sure they were immortals." His wife was not convinced. "What is it about them that makes you think they were immortals?" Wang then described how only after walking a few miles they had arrived at a bridge some twenty miles away, how a table of wine and food had been prepared in a desolate place, and how he had climbed the mountain to the lake where the lotus flowers bloomed. His wife listened and said, "You said you only drank a few cups of wine. How come you were so drunk that you totally lost consciousness? That was no normal wine. I have heard that there are robbers who put sleeping potions into wine to get people drunk after one or two cups. Then they rob them of their money and goods, leaving them lying drunk on the wayside. I have also heard that such thieves know some magic and in no time at all can transport you to a place far from where they have drugged you. The world is full of evil people. Beware of them! You have such a good and trusting nature that I am afraid that you are easily deceived. Promise me that you will be careful in the future." Wang thought to himself, "My wife has good intentions, but she does not understand the mysterious ways of the immortals. I shall let the matter rest and not argue with her." So he said aloud, "You are right. I should be more careful about my behavior in the future."

Wang could not keep the events of the past few days off his mind. He spent his time alone in his study, trying to decipher the meaning of his meeting with the beggars, who he was certain were immortals. One day it suddenly occurred to him that the identities of the beggars were hidden in their names. The first beggar was named Gold-Is-Heavy. If the Chinese characters for "gold" and "heavy" were put together they formed the word *Chung*. As for Empty-Mind Ch'ang, if the Chinese character *ch'ang* were to lose the strokes in the center (that is, "emptying its heart or mind"), it would become the word *lü*. *Chung* and *Lü* were the beggars' real names. Clearly, Chung and Lü were Chung-li Ch'üan and Lü Tung-pin, two of the famous Eight Immortals. Wang exclaimed to himself, "I met two of the greatest immortals and did not recognize them there and then. How stupid of me! Yet before they left, they said that we would meet again soon. And they said that it would be in three months. This is the twelfth month. They must have meant that we should meet again in the third month of the new year. I must not miss this appointment."

Winter passed, and it was spring. On the third day of the third month Wang secretly left home and journeyed twenty miles to the bridge where he had bid farewell to the two immortals. He sat by the bridge and waited patiently, looking around from time to time to make sure he did not miss any traveler passing through

萬緣橋真傳
妙道
大魏村假裝
中風
長沙郭子枢

Master Wang and the two beggars meet at the bridge. In his mansion Master Wang pretends to be ill with an incurable disease.

9

the area. Suddenly he heard someone call his name; looking behind him, he saw his two old friends dressed in rags. They laughed and said, "Master Wang has not only kept his appointment but arrived early!" Gold-Is-Heavy and Empty-Mind Ch'ang walked toward the bridge. Wang immediately dropped to his knees before them and bowed many times. "Great Immortals, it is a honor to see you again. Forgive my stupidity and my inability to recognize who you were when we last met. Today I am fortunate to see you again, and I hope you will instruct me and lead me to the Tao."

The two beggars laughed heartily. Wang could see an aura of light surrounding them. Their eyes shone brilliantly, and their look penetrated his entire being. Suddenly the two beggars were transformed into two men with striking appearances. One was dressed in a simple short tunic and pants. His tunic opened to reveal a tuft of hair on his chest. The hair on his head was neatly tied into two knots next to his ears. His beard was long and flowing. He held a goose-feather fan and carried a gourd on his back. This was none other than the immortal Chung-li Ch'üan. The other man was dressed in a long yellow Taoist robe. Around his topknot was tied a scarf. His face was rosy and shiny. His beard was long and jet black. His gaze was penetrating and his composure stately. Tied around his back was a long sword to cut through the illusions of ephemeral things. He was the Patriarch of Pure Yang, Immortal Lü Tung-pin. Wang immediately prostrated himself. Immortal Lü said, "In the ancient days, people were honest and humble. Therefore the Immortals taught their disciples magical powers before teaching them techniques of internal alchemy. In these times, people do not have such strong willpower. I am afraid that if they were given instructions in Taoist magic, they would use them for personal power and forget about the cultivation of the heart and body. As a result they would end by being still further from attaining the Tao. We shall teach you the methods of internal alchemy first. When your heart and body are transformed, there will be no magical feat that you cannot perform. Cultivate your heart, for only your original heart can see what is real. These are the teachings of the real truth. Remember them well."

Immortal Lü then imparted to Wang the principles and methods of internal alchemy:

"The real is that which is true and not false. Every person has a true heart. If the true heart strays, however, then it becomes untrue to its own nature. Every person has a true intention. But if the true intention strays, it becomes untrue to its own nature. Every person has a true feeling. When the true feeling strays from the original nature, it becomes untrue. An intention that originates from the true heart is true intention. The intention that is calculating and scheming is untrue. A feeling that originates from the true heart is true feeling. Feeling that has self-importance in it is untrue. What is the true heart? The true heart is original nature. The true heart tends toward goodness. Feeling and intention originate from the heart. If the heart is true, the feeling and intention will be true. Cultivating the true heart is cultivating original nature. Original nature is the manifestation of the natural way of Heaven. Many who claim to cultivate the Tao still possess egotistical thoughts. Where there is ego, the true heart cannot emerge. It is only in stillness and the absence of craving that original nature can be cultivated. Those who seek the Tao must begin with knowing the difference between true and untrue feeling, true and untrue intention. If you know the difference, then you will know the true heart. Intention and feeling can be known by observing the behavior in your daily life. If your actions are not sincere, then true feeling is absent. If your words are false, then true intention is absent. If you want to cultivate the Tao you must eradicate attachments that lead true intention and true feeling astray. Let original nature rather than your ego guide your actions. Do not waver in your pursuit of goodness. Then, your true heart, true feeling, and true intention will emerge and you will not be far from the Tao. These are the teachings of the real truth."

Immortal Lü then taught Wang the methods of "erecting the foundation," "positioning the cauldron and the stove," "stoking the fires," and "gathering the herbs and sealing the container." Wang bowed low and thanked the immortals many times. Immortal Lü then said to him, "After you have attained the Tao, you should go to Shantung Province and gather the seven disciples who are destined to be guided by you to the Tao. Remember the seven golden lotus flowers entrusted to your care." The two immortals were transformed into a beam of bright light and disappeared. Wang stood deep in thought for a long time until he heard footsteps behind him. He turned and saw two of his servants running toward him, saying, "When the mistress found that you had been gone all day she sent us looking for you. She was afraid you might have run into danger. Master, please come home with us now so the mistress will not be worried." Wang followed the servants home, pondering the words and instructions of the two immortals.

Arriving at the mansion, Wang went immediately into his study and closed the door. His wife, hearing that her husband had returned, went to the study and found Wang sitting silently and deep in thought. She spoke to him gently. "Husband, you were away all day, wandering about aimlessly. If your strange behavior is noticed by the people of the village you will lose your reputation and be the laugh of the town. What am I to do?" All this time Wang was thinking about Immortal Lü's instructions regarding internal alchemy. He was totally unaware of his wife's presence until he heard her say, "What am I to do?" Startled, Wang stared at his wife and mumbled, "What am I to do? What am I to do?" Seeing Wang confused and unlike his normal self, his wife silently left the room.

When Wang was alone he said to himself, "If I am disturbed like this all the time, how will I find the concentration and time to practice internal alchemy? I need to come up with a plan to isolate myself from the mundane affairs of the world." He thought for a long time and finally devised a plan. Pretending to have suffered a stroke, he acted as if he had lost his memory and speech. He uttered nonsense and groaned frequently as if he were in pain. Often he would simply lay on his bed, staring at nothing. Seeing Wang's condition, his wife was worried and upset. She asked some of Wang's closest friends to visit, hoping that they might discover what had happened to her husband. As soon as Wang's friends saw him they asked about his condition. Wang shook his head, groaned again, waved his arms about, and sighed. When his friends saw that Wang had trouble speaking, they agreed that he was ill. One of the friends, an elderly gentleman, said, "I am afraid our friend must have had a mild stroke. It appears that he has lost his speech and his memory. I know of a famous doctor from a village east of here who might be able to cure him. We should invite the doctor to come here and have a look at Master Wang's condition." Hearing this, Wang's wife immediately sent a servant to accompany the doctor to the Wang mansion.

The doctor examined Wang and found that his pulse was normal and that there were no signs of illness except for Wang's strange behavior. Finally the doctor said, "Master Wang has suffered a mild stroke. I shall prescribe some medicine for him. He should recover soon."

3

When Wang's friends had left, his son went to purchase the prescribed medicine from the village herb shop. The bowl of herbs was brought to Wang, but when he saw his son he rolled his eyes and made threatening gestures toward the boy. The boy left the bowl on the table and ran as fast as he could from the study. From then on, no one but Wang's personal servant could enter the study. The other servants were utterly afraid of Wang's volatile behavior. His wife made frequent visits initially, but Wang pretended to be in a stupor whenever she appeared. After several months it appeared that Wang was not about to make a speedy "recovery."

After Wang fell into his mock illness he disengaged himself entirely from the family business. His wife now took over the management of the business and the day-to-day affairs at home and had little time to visit her husband. Relatives and friends began to get used to Wang's "illness" and erratic behavior and left him alone. Most of them simply accepted the state of affairs and said, "It is a pity that a man in his prime, one with fame and fortune, should be struck with an incurable disease."

Wang was now left in peace to practice internal alchemy. He was visited only by his personal servant, who brought him food three times a day. This went on for twelve years, during which time Wang was able to achieve the internal transformation that allowed his spirit to leave and enter his body by will. Knowing that he had completed his training, Wang gave himself a Taoist name: Wang Ch'ung-yang. *"Ch'ung yang"* means recovering the essence of *yang*.

One day as he was meditating, he heard a clear voice calling his name. The voice said, "Wang Ch'ung-yang, ascend to the heavens immediately for instructions from the Heavenly Lords." Wang's spirit ascended to heaven and saw the Lord of the Star T'ai-pa (White Tiger) standing there to greet him. He bowed low, and the scribe of the Heavenly Lord read from a scroll: "Wang Ch'ung-yang, your efforts of cultivating the Tao are acknowledged by the Guardians of the Tao. You have attained the fruit of cultivation and have achieved the status of an immortal. You are given the title "Enlightened Master who Opens the Way." Go to Shantung Province immediately and find the seven persons who are destined to be your disciples. When you have helped them attain the Tao, your rank in the immortal realm will be raised."

Wang Ch'ung-yang thanked the Heavenly Lords and the Guardians of the Tao. The Lord of T'ai-pa added, "Enlightened One, you must hurry to Shantung immediately to help the people to return to the Tao. Your name is "One who Opens the Way." The karma of many rests on your efforts. We shall meet again at the gathering of the immortals when the Empress of Heaven summons us to taste the peach of immortality."

The next morning, the servant who brought Wang's breakfast found the door of the study locked. The servant knocked many times but there was no answer. Fearing that Wang might have died or that he was unconscious, the servant roused the household. Wang's wife and son hurried to the study and called loudly for Wang to open the door. Finally, the servants broke the lock and opened the door. The study was empty. Wang had disappeared. Servants were sent around the village to look for him, but he could not be found. Wang's wife wept and mourned. The commotion at the Wang mansion soon lured curious neighbors, friends, and relatives to ask what had happened. Wang's servant explained, "This morning when I brought the master his breakfast, the door of the study was locked. When we went in, the room was empty. There is no hole in the roof, and I usually sit by the door to attend to the master's needs. Our master has disappeared mysteriously." An elderly man in the crowd said, "You need not look for Master Wang. I think he has become an immortal and has ascended to Heaven." A number of people voiced disbelief, but the old man continued, speaking to Wang's servant, "Have you not noticed the complexion and the appearance of your master? A sick man does not have rosy cheeks and bright eyes. Has he aged in the twelve years of isolation in his study?" The servant could only admit that the old man was right. His master had behaved strangely, but in no way had his com-

受天詔
山東度
世入地
終南道
藏身
子桓

Wang Ch'ung-yang attains the Tao and is commanded by the Lords
of Heaven to spread the teachings of the Tao in Shantung.
Wang Ch'ung-yang hides in a cave in Mount Chung-nan
and is rebuked by Immortal Lü and Immortal Chung-li Ch'üan.

plexion resembled that of a sick man. Moreover, over the years Wang had hardly aged. In fact, one might say that he had actually gotten younger and more robust. The old man said, "Now you understand. Master Wang pretended to be ill all these years so he could be alone and cultivate himself to become an immortal. Do not look for him any longer. He has probably left the earthly realm." The crowd filed away. Some believed the old man's explanation of Wang's disappearance. Others doubted. But all agreed it was a mystery how a man could disappear through solid walls and guarded doors.

On the day of his disappearance from his home, Wang used his magical abilities to pass through walls and journey under the ground until he was far from his village. He started traveling eastward to Shantung Province to find his seven disciples. He journeyed thousands of miles, but on the road he met only two kinds of people: those who desired fame and those who desired riches. No one was interested in what he had to teach about the Tao. Seeing the apathetic attitude of the people, he returned to Shensi Province. Passing by an area known as Mount Chung-nan, he was taken by the beautiful landscape of rolling hills, wooded slopes, and hidden waterfalls. He decided to stay here as a hermit and wait for the time when people would be ready to accept the Tao. Tunnelling into a hill, he found a cave. There he lay down, brought his breath under control, and, like an animal hibernating in winter, slowed down his bodily functions, conserving the energy for the day he would emerge from the cave.

Wang had been in the cave for half a year when one day he heard a loud sound. The earth shook and a large crack split his cave open, revealing a shaft of bright light from the sky. The beam of light slowly transformed itself into the figures of Immortal Lü and Immortal Chung-li Ch'üan. Immortal Lü laughed and said, "When people become immortal, they ascend to the heavens. How come when you became immortal, you hid underground? It looks like you haven't been doing what you were supposed to do." Wang Ch'ung-yang knelt before his teachers and said humbly, "I did not mean to disobey the orders of the Heavenly Lords and my teachers. I journeyed to Shantung and found nobody willing to listen to my teachings. Thus I thought that the time was not ripe and I should lie here and wait until there would be people willing to accept the Tao." Immortal Lü said, "There are people waiting for you everywhere. You could not find them because you did not know how to look. Take yourself, for instance. You were destined to attain the Tao, yet we could not have found you had we not disguised ourselves as beggars traveling around the countryside. If we had simply looked around we would never have found you. Do you understand now? Everyone is ready to accept the Tao. It is up to you to find the right opportunity to teach them."

Immortal Lü continued. "I was in the city of Loyang and found that there was no opportunity for me to teach the people there. So I went to the kingdom of Chin, a land of so-called barbarians. There I found the prime minister of the kingdom to be a virtuous man, and I imparted to him the teachings of the Tao. This man immediately resigned his office, left his fiefdom, and followed me into the mountains. He has now attained the Tao and has been given the Taoist name Liu Hai-ch'an. Liu journeyed south and gave the teachings to Chang Tzu-yang. Chang Tzu-yang became the patriarch of the Southern School of Taoism. From the seven lines of transmission which originated from him came the Seven Taoist Masters of the Southern School. For Chang Tzu-yang taught Hou Hsing-lin. Hou Hsing-lin transmitted the teachings to Hsüeh Tao-kuang. Hsüeh Tao-kuang taught Chen Chih-hsü. Chen Chih-hsü taught Pai Tzu-ch'ing. Pai Tzu-ch'ing gave the teachings to Liu Yung-nien and Pang Ho-lin. From them the teachings of the Tao blossomed in the south, and each was responsible for imparting the teachings of the Tao to many. And here you are, saying that there is no one to be taught. Your seven disciples are destined for immortality. They will form the Northern School of Taoism and be known as the Seven Taoist Masters of the Northern School. You should learn from the example of Liu Hai-ch'an, for your abilities are not inferior to his." When Wang Ch'ung-yang heard this, he trembled in fear and remained prostrated on the ground.

Immortal Chung-li Ch'üan directed him to stand up and said kindly, "Do you know why we are pressing you to hurry and help the Northern Seven Masters to attain immortality? It is because the meeting of the immortals in the celebration of the flowering of the immortal peach is imminent. The peach tree grows on the mountain K'un-lun, where it flowers once every thousand years. It fertilizes a seed once every thousand years, and the seed ripens into a fruit once every thousand years. Three thousand years must pass before a fruit of the peach tree ripens. The ripened peach is large as a melon, red, and shiny, and even one bite of it would lengthen your life by one thousand years. The Empress of Heaven does not want to eat the fruit all by herself but has invited all those whose names are entered in the roll of the immortals to share the fruit. The Seven Taoist Masters of the Northern School are on the invitation list, but in order to attend the celebration they must have attained the Tao by then. If those invited do not attend, the Empress of Heaven will be very disappointed. In the first era of humankind, a thousand mortals attained immortality. In the second era, a few hundred will achieve immortality. These immortals will return to the earthly realm to help others leave the wheel of reincarnation after their deeds are acknowledged by the Empress of Heaven at the celebration. If you are unable to help your seven disciples attain the Tao by the time of the celebration, many mortals will have to wait another three thousand years before their teacher will appear."

Wang Ch'ung-yang finally understood. Humbly he said, "My heart was clouded. Now it is clear. I shall go to Shantung and search for my seven disciples." Immortal Chung-li Ch'üan added, "Remember, go to where the land meets the sea, where horses are plenty and towns nestle in the rolling hills." The two immortals disappeared and Wang immediately set out for Shantung Province. He journeyed to a county called Ning-hai (meaning "settlement by the sea") and remembered Immortal Chung-li Ch'üan's words, "Go to where the land meets the sea." There he halted his travels. Dressed like a beggar—like Immortal Lü and Immortal Chung-li Ch'üan—he entered a town and mingled with the people.

4

In the county of Ning-hai lived a wealthy family who belonged to the Ma clan. The master of the family was called Ma Yü. His parents had died when he was young, and being the only child, he grew up alone. He inherited the family business, married a beautiful and intelligent woman named Sun Yüan-chen and settled into a quiet and comfortable life in the Ma mansion. Sun Yüan-chen was a remarkable woman. She was gentle and calm in her disposition, loved to study the classics, and appreciated simple living even though the Ma family was extremely rich. She preferred painting, calligraphy, and writing poetry to sewing and other typical womanly activities. Unlike most women of her time, she participated actively in managing the family estate and often advised her husband on business matters. Ma Yü respected his wife's intelligence and welcomed her participation in making decisions. The couple enjoyed each other's company, for they shared common intellectual interests. Their relationship was one of mutual caring and respect. Everything seemed perfect except that they had no children, and now they were both approaching forty.

One day as the autumn leaves were falling, Ma Yü and Sun Yüan-chen were sitting in a pavilion in the garden. Ma Yü suddenly sighed and said to his wife, "We are both approaching forty, and we have no son to carry on the family line and take care of the family business. I wonder what will happen to all our hard work after we die?" Sun Yüan-chen replied, "The works of the Three Emperors, the heroes Yü and Shun, the Seven Warlords, Liu Pei and his renowned strategist K'ung Ming, all the emperors of dynasties gone by, are now nothing. What have they left that was lasting? The treasures of the emperors far surpass ours, but still eventually they are dust. Material things are impermanent. Why should we worry so much about what may happen to them?" Ma Yü laughed good-naturedly and said, "Even if material things are impermanent, at least others have sons to carry on the family line. As for us, we are truly empty of everything." Sun Yüan-chen said, "We are not truly empty, for to be truly empty one must find the source of true emptiness." She continued, "If we think that having descendants will make our existence permanent, we need only to look at Emperor Wen of the Chou dynasty. It was said that he had a hundred sons. How many people have you met who carry his family name of Chi? Look at other famous large families of old. Many of them have no descendants to visit their graves. Look at the burial grounds: many graves are unattended. Even if we had sons and daughters, we would not know what will happen after we die. Why worry about things which we cannot see and cannot know? You and I have lived happy years. We are rich, but one can only eat so much a day and sleep so much at night. When we are asleep we are oblivious to what we are sleeping on. Riches and fortune cannot buy us a reprieve from death. We shall all die one day, rich and poor alike."

Sun Yüan-chen continued. "We should make better use of the years left to us. Rather than sit and worry about what may happen after we die, we should seek out a teacher who can lead us to the path of immortality so our spirits will be freed from the earthly realm." Ma Yü replied, "The methods of attaining immortality are just legends. Everyone grows old and dies. That which begins must have an end." But Sun Yüan-chen said, "Husband, listen to me. I am not very learned, but I have read a few Taoist classics of internal alchemy. They describe how the generative energy can be transformed into vital energy, how the vital energy can be transformed into spiritual energy, how the spirit can be cultivated to return to the void, and how the void can be cultivated to merge with the Tao. This is the path of immortality." Ma Yü said, "How can one form of energy be transformed into another? This does not make sense." Sun Yüan-chen said, "The methods of transformation are taught by enlightened masters who have undergone the transformations themselves. If you want to know more, you must search for a teacher to guide you." Ma Yü then said, "My wife, you are intelligent and know much. I shall ask you to be my teacher, and you will teach me these things." Sun Yüan-chen replied, "Husband, my learning is shallow. I have only read a few books. I am not qualified to be your teacher. We

談真空
孫貞誨
夫主求
妙道馬
鈺訪明
師 郁子和

Sun Yüan-chen and Ma Yü discuss the teachings of the Tao and decide to seek a teacher

should try and find a Taoist master to teach us." Ma Yü said, "I would gladly search for a teacher, but I am afraid I do not have the foundation to learn Taoist internal alchemy. They say that those who attempt Taoist training must already have a strong and deep foundation. I do not even have the faintest idea of what Taoist training involves." But Sun Yüan-chen said, "The fact that we are in human form shows that we have the foundation. One who had not accumulated good works in previous lifetimes would not take on human form in this lifetime. Whether a foundation is shallow or deep can be seen in a person's mental ability, physical condition, and fortune. Those with shallow foundations may be born ill of health, lack intelligence, or be born into poor families or suffer deformities. Those with deep and strong foundations will be born with good health, possess high intelligence, and be born into wealth and comfort. However, foundations are not solely dependent on deeds in previous lifetimes. One may also strengthen the foundation by performing good deeds in the current lifetime. Likewise, a strong foundation may be eroded by evil deeds performed in this lifetime. Husband, you were born into a wealthy family and blessed with good health. This shows that your foundation is strong."

Ma Yü was a person with spiritual leanings. Now that he had heard his wife's analysis of the matter he thanked her many times and said, "Let us go and look for a teacher immediately. But where shall we begin?" Sun Yüan-chen said, "That should not be too difficult. I have seen an old man who often begs in this town. From his appearance I can see that he is not an ordinary man. His eyes shine radiantly. His face is rosy, and despite his age his hair is black. He must be an enlightened person. Why don't we invite him here and ask him to be our teacher?" Ma Yü said, "Good. Let us look for him. Even if he is not a Taoist master, we should offer a beggar a place to stay."

During the years Wang Ch'ung-yang had stayed at Ning-hai County, he had continued to refine his magical abilities and internal cultivation. He was now able to see into the future and anticipate many happenings. He was able to see into people's hearts and evaluate the strength of their foundation and their chances of success in attaining the Tao. He now realized what Immortal Ch'ung-li Ch'üan had meant when he said, "Look where there are plenty of horses." (The word for "horse" in Chinese is *ma*, as in the family name of Ma Yü.) He knew that the gathering of his seven disciples would begin with Ma Yü and his wife. Therefore he stayed close to the Ma mansion, patiently waiting for the chance to come. He had seen Ma Yü from a distance several times and knew him to be a virtuous man. He had seen Sun Yüan-chen twice and knew that she possessed a phenomenal intelligence. He had not approached them because he felt that if Ma Yü and his wife did not make the first gesture, the meeting would be forced. Thus all these years he had made his appearance as a beggar at a crossroad not far from the Ma mansion. The townspeople saw only a beggar, but Sun Yüan-chen was no ordinary woman. She saw in him the teacher who would guide her and her husband to the immortal realm. It is said that out of Wang Ch'ung-yang's group of seven disciples, Sun Yüan-chen attained the highest level of internal cultivation.

After Ma Yü and Sun Yüan-chen decided to ask the old beggar to be their teacher, Ma Yü posted a servant in front of his home and instructed him to report at once when the old beggar appeared. One day, when Ma Yü was sitting in the living room waiting for news of the beggar, the servant ran in saying that the beggar had been seen across the street. When Ma Yü heard this he immediately got up and hurried to the front door.

5

If one wants to attain enlightenment, one must begin by cultivating the heart [or mind]. If the heart is true, the body will be healthy and all one's action will be virtuous. If the heart is untrue, the body will be unhealthy and all one's actions will be without virtue. This is why those who are attempting to cultivate the Tao in themselves begin with taming the heart. When the heart is tamed, the intentions will be sincere. If the heart is not tamed, the intentions will be insincere and desire and craving will rise. As a result, the Tao will be lost forever. The ancient sages said, "When untamed thoughts arise, the spirit will leave. When the spirit leaves, the Six Theives—eyes, ears, mouth, nose, body, thoughts—will disrupt the heart. When the heart is disrupted, the body has no center and you will be doomed to reincarnation. You may become an animal, a hungry ghost, or a wandering soul. Do not let your thoughts lead you astray or else you will be sunk into ten thousand karmic retributions." The difference between mortals and immortals lies in whether the heart is true and void of untamed thoughts. If your heart is not tamed, no matter how frequently you chant the scriptures or make offerings to the Heavenly Lords, you will not be able to attain enlightenment.

Ma Yü invited the beggar, who was really Wang Ch'ung-yang, into his mansion. Wang Ch'ung-yang strode into the living room, sat down, and said in a haughty voice, "You asked me to come, now what do you want?" Respectfully Ma Yü said, "I saw you begging at the street corner. An old man like you should at least spend the rest of your days sheltered from the elements and be assured of hot meals. I would like to invite you to stay at my mansion. In this way, your needs will be taken care of." Wang Ch'ung-yang replied rudely, "I would rather beg then ask you to provide for me the rest of my life." Seeing that the old man was angered, Ma Yü was afraid to ask any more. He quietly went to the study, found his wife, and described the situation to her, "The old beggar was angry when I told him that I would gladly provide for his needs the rest of his life. It looks like he is not going to stay. What are we to do?" Sun Yüan-chen smiled and said, "The enlightened person thinks of spiritual matters. The unenlightened person thinks of material matters. You offered him material comfort. No wonder he got angry. He probably thought that you were trying to entice him with material goods. Let me go and speak with him. I think I know what to say to make him stay."

Sun Yüan-chen came into the living room and bowed low to Wang Ch'ung-yang. "Sir, prosperity and fortune are with you." The old beggar laughed and said, "I am a beggar. What is it that makes me prosperous and fortunate?" Sun Yüan-chen said, "Sir, you have no worries and no attachments. You wander in freedom and leisure. No material goods hold you. Is this not fortune? Your heart is clear and calm. You are not disturbed by craving and desire. Is this not prosperity? Many people think they are fortunate when they are rich, but they do not know that riches imprison them. Many think that they are prosperous, but they spend their time worrying about losing their wealth. In the end, when they die, they cannot take their so-called fortune and prosperity with them. Sir, your prosperity and fortune, on the other hand, are eternal. They cannot be taken away; and they will not decay." The old beggar laughed and said, "Well said! To be free of attachment is fortune. To be clear and calm of mind is prosperity. Why haven't you learned to clear your mind and dissolve your attachments?" Sun Yüan-chen answered, "I would like to, but there is no one to teach me." Wang Ch'ung-yang said, "If you are willing to learn, I shall teach you." Sun Yüan-chen then thanked him and said, "Sir, we are grateful that you are willing to teach us. In the back garden is a spacious room. It is quiet there. Please make yourself comfortable. We shall come and study with you there."

Wang Ch'ung-yang was pleased with Sun Yüan-chen's behavior and accepted her invitation. A room was cleaned out, furniture was moved in, and a servant was assigned to attend to Wang Ch'ung-yang's needs. When all was prepared and Wang Ch'ung-yang had settled into his room, Ma Yü said to Sun Yüan-chen, "All this time we have talked with our teacher and I have

馬員外勤奉養
師禮
王重陽經營護
道財

子桓 〔印〕

Ma Yü asks Wang Ch'ung-yang to be his teacher. Wang Ch'ung-yang
requires him to give up his wealth and property.

27

forgotten to ask him his name. I should go and find out who he is." His wife said, "The enlightened do not attach themselves to a name. It really does not matter whether we know his name or not." But Ma Yü was curious and decided to ask the beggar his name.

Ma Yü arrived at the back garden and saw the old man meditating on the bed in his room. Slowly he pushed open the door, walked toward the meditating man, and asked, "Sir, if it is permitted, may I ask your name, where you are from, and why you have journeyed to this area?" The old man slowly opened his eyes and said curtly, "My name is Wang Ch'ung-yang. I am from Shensi Province. And I came here because of you." Ma Yü was stunned. He stammered, "Sir, you came here because of me?" Wang Ch'ung-yang clapped his hands and said, "That's right. I came here because you are here." Ma Yü then asked, "How is it that you come because of me?" Wang Ch'ung-yang replied, "I came because of your wealth." When Ma Yü heard this he was astonished. "If you come because of my wealth, then are you saying that you want my wealth?" Wang Ch'ung-yang said, "If I didn't want your wealth, why would I travel so far from Shensi to here?" Ma Yü was beginning to get annoyed. He tried to speak, could find nothing to say, and walked out of the room.

Ma Yü left the back garden muttering to himself, "That beggar is outrageous. He wants my property and wealth, and he had the gall to say so in front of me! And he claims to be an enlightened man!" He went into the study without saying a word to his wife and sat down. Sun Yüan-chen noticed her husband's behavior and knew something was wrong. She said gently, "You must have asked the old man his name, and he must have been irritated by your questioning. Now you are annoyed because he said something that offended you." Ma Yü calmed down and said, "I thought that old man was enlightened and virtuous. But just now he had the nerve to ask me to give him our wealth!" Sun Yüan-chen said, "The old gentleman must have had a reason when he asked for your wealth. Maybe you should ask him what it is. Husband, the land and property we own, even the trees in the garden and the rice in the fields, are not really our own. They belong to the land, and the land belongs to everyone. We were merely given the opportunity to be caretakers for a while. During one lifetime we may have much, in another lifetime we may have nothing. Riches come and go. You said Master Wang wanted our wealth. If he has a legitimate reason, why not give it to him? We have no children. Our wealth has to go to someone even if we do not give it away." Ma Yü interjected, "Woman, it is easy for you to say these things. But I have a responsibility to my ancestors who left me this heritage. Our wealth was built up from the hard work of ancestors who migrated from Shensi. How can I just give it to somebody I hardly know? Besides, we are only middle-aged. If we forfeit our wealth, then how will we support ourselves for the rest of our lives?" Sun Yüan-chen said, "We are seeking the path of immortality. When we have attained the Tao, what need will we have for this wealth? And it is said that if a person becomes an immortal, the karma of nine generations is swept clean. Cultivation of ourselves will help our ancestors leave the wheel of reincarnation. This is much better than preserving material goods that they cannot enjoy." Ma Yü disagreed. "If we become immortal, then things will be fine. But suppose we do not? Then we will have squandered all our wealth. We will have achieved nothing and lost everything." His wife answered patiently, "The sages say that to cultivate immortality one must be sincere and ready to make sacrifices. Even acquiring the skills of divination and medicine requires sincerity and sacrifice. The cultivation of immortality is no simple task. It will require of us more sacrifice than any other undertaking." She continued, "It is within the ability of each individual to cultivate the Tao. Success or failure depends on whether the sincerity and sacrifice are there. The bodhisattvas and the Taoist immortals were all mortals once." Ma Yü said to his wife, "You are right. I shall ask the old man why he wanted our wealth."

The next morning Ma Yü found Wang Ch'ung-yang and asked, "Sir, yesterday you said you wanted my wealth. May I ask what are the reasons?" Wang Ch'ung-yang replied, "I need your wealth to construct a retreat for seekers of the Tao. Your wealth will also provide for the daily necessities of these people so that they will not have to worry about earning a living and can devote all their time to Taoist training." When Ma Yü heard the answer he was finally satisfied and asked no more.

6

When Ma Yü understood that Wang Ch'ung-yang wanted his wealth to build a retreat he said, "Sir, you are a truly
enlightened person. My wife and I would like to become your
disciples." Wang Chung-yang said, "If the two of you are willing
to learn, I shall accept you as disciples. But first you must arrange
to transfer all your wealth to me." Ma Yü said, "Sir, you are free
to use my wealth any time you wish and whichever way you want.
Why do we need to go through the formalities of transferring our
property, our money, and our business holdings to you?" Wang
Ch'ung-yang replied; "As long as you hold titles to your property
and business, your mind will still be attached to them. If you
sign them away you will find that it is easier for you to forget
about worldly attachments." Ma Yü said, "That is fine. I shall
deliver the deeds of my properties and the accounts of my
business to your safekeeping." But Wang Ch'ung-yang said, "In
order for the transfer of property and business holdings to be
complete, you need to sign a document stating that you have
transferred your possessions to me at your own free will. The
signing will have to be witnessed by your relatives and the head
of your family clan." [Chinese formality requires that if family
possessions are to be transferred to persons outside the clan, the
transfer must be verbally agreed on by the closest relatives and
witnessed and endorsed with signatures from three clan members, one of them being the clan leader.]

When Ma Yü heard this he was worried. To involve the family
clan was something he did not look forward to, for he anticipated
trouble. He consulted with Sun Yüan-chen. "Master Wang wants
me to will all our possessions to him formally. I am afraid our
relatives will oppose this. Many of them have their eyes on our
possessions. We have no heirs. They all expect to get a piece of
our wealth when we die. If they hear that I am planning to give
everything away to an unknown and unrelated old man, they will
do everything to oppose it." Sun Yüan-chen said, "I think you
should first present your idea to the prominent members of the

family clan and the closest relatives. If they agree with your actions, then everything is fine. If they don't, I have a plan that will guarantee that the clan elders will support your actions and the transfer of our possessions to Master Wang will be a success."

Ma Yü immediately dispatched servants to invite his granduncles, uncles, cousins, and nephews for a dinner at the mansion. On the appointed day the relatives arrived. In the group was an elderly clan member, Ma Lung, who was a granduncle of Ma Yü. He had held a government post before retirement and was the eldest member of the clan. He approached Ma Yü and asked, "What is the occasion for this clan gathering?" Ma Yü answered, "Granduncle, my health has been deteriorating these years. Two out of every three days I feel tired. I am afraid that I do not have the energy to take care of my estate and business. My wife is also frail and weak and has neither the skill nor inclination to take over the task. Recently I met a sincere and honest man. I have invited him to live at my home, and I plan to transfer my business and properties to him so he can help me take care of them. The reason for inviting all of you here today is to sign the transfer formally with witnesses in front of the family clan." One of the cousins overheard this and was outraged. In a loud voice he exclaimed, "Ma Yü, you must be mad! The property and business of our ancestors should be kept in the family clan. How can you transfer them to someone outside our family? Who duped you into doing this thing?" Ma Yü knew Ma Ming was hotheaded and could cause much trouble. Not wanting to make matters worse, he pretended to be attentive to other relatives and walked away from him. Another powerful clan member, Ma Wen-fui, who overheard the conversation, said, "Ma Ming, your cousin Ma Yü is known to be an honest and careful man. I have not seen him make mistakes as far as his finances are concerned. Before you argue with him, let us ask this Master Wang to come out and meet us. I would like to find out what kind of person Ma Yü has willed his possessions to." Ma Wen-fui was an uncle of Ma Yü. Before retirement he had held a post in the Imperial Academy in the Capital and had been responsible for tutoring the sons of the nobility. His word was respected, and decisions about clan matters were often entrusted to him.

孫淵貞勸夫捨家財
馬文魁受略通權變
于桓

Sun Yüan-chen persuades Ma Yü to give up his wealth and property. Clan leader Ma Wen-fui is bribed and persuaded to support Ma Yü's decision to transfer his wealth to Wang Ch'ung-yang.

32

When Wang Ch'ung-yang entered the room, he did not even greet Ma Yü's relatives. Ma Wen-fui said to him, "I see you are the old man who begs at the crossroad near this mansion. My nephew Ma Yü has been kind enough to provide you with food and shelter and even spending money. Why aren't you satisfied? Why do you want him to sign over his business and his estate to you? You are over sixty years old, yet you haven't learned what shame means." Wang Ch'ung-yang said nonchalantly, "I am sick of being poor all my life. I want to live the rest of my days in luxury. What is so shameful about that?" Hearing the old man's rebuttal to a clan elder, two young nephews of Ma Yü pushed their way from behind the crowd, spat at Wang Ch'ung-yang, and said, "You disrespectful old rascal! You are only a beggar and you are not even from our county. How dare you mess with our clan and speak such shameful words in front of well-respected leaders of the community!" Turning to the other relatives, they said, "We are wasting our time with this scoundrel. Let us run him out of town at once!" They were about to lay hold of Wang Ch'ung-yang when a stately-looking man stepped out and barred their way. Ma Liu was a cousin of Ma Yü. He too held a government appointment and was a prominent member in the clan. Ma Liu said, "We should not run this old man out of town. He is homeless and poor. Charity demands that we be kind to him. Ma Yü has invited him to stay at his mansion. We should not interfere with this charitable deed. However, I think that Ma Yü should not transfer his business holdings and estates to the old man." The young men quieted down. As Ma Yü had anticipated, the transfer of his possessions to Wang Chung-yang was not going to be smooth.

During dinner, Ma Yü whispered a few words to his cousin Ma Liu, and Ma Liu spoke briefly and quietly to Ma Lung and Ma Wen-fui, the other two clan leaders. Ma Wen-fui stood up and spoke to the relatives. "With respect to Ma Yu's proposal of transferring his possessions to Wang Ch'ung-yang, I have discussed the matter with Ma Lung and Ma Liu. We thought that it would be better if the three of us represent the clan and talk to Ma Yü about the matter under more peaceful and quiet circumstances. In the meantime I ask you all to go home after dinner

33

and trust the matter to us." The three men commanded high respect within the clan, and no one disputed Ma Wen-fui's proposal. Ma Lung was the nominal leader of the clan, but Ma Wen-fui held the real power in making decisions and was the chief spokesman of the clan. Ma Liu was the most shrewd and had the power in swaying opinion of clan members. If these three men supported Ma Yü's plan of action, most likely none of the other relatives would oppose it.

After the relatives had left, Ma Yü, Ma Wen-fui, Ma Liu, and Ma Lung retired into the study. Soon, a servant brought in wine and fruits. After a few cups, Ma Yü stood up respectfully and said, "I have a few things on my mind that I wish to share, and I hope my granduncle, uncle, and cousin can help me solve my problems. I owe my gratitude to our ancestors. Normally I would not dare to transfer my possessions to one who does not share our family name. However, my health has not been good these past years, and I wish to take a few years away from the worries of managing the business so that I may get a chance to recover. In the meantime, Wang Ch'ung-yang will take care of the business affairs. I plan to reclaim my possessions when my health allows me to take an active part in managing the business." Ma Liu said, "Cousin, if this is the case you need not sign over your possessions formally. Just give Wang Ch'ung-yang your account-ing records and property deeds for temporary safekeeping." Ma Yü said, "A man will not put his whole heart in an undertaking if it is not his own. If I transfer my possessions to Master Wang formally, he will feel that he is managing his own business and will not be careless with our wealth." Ma Lung said, "I do not follow this logic."

Ma Yü said, "Let me tell you the whole situation. I asked Master Wang to take care of my business while I recover my health. This old man is very honest and down-to-earth. I told him to look after my business affairs with care and that he should treat them as his own. What I meant was that he should take the attitude of 'do for others as if you were doing it for yourself.' The old man misunderstood and thought that I was going to sign my possessions over to him. Immediately he asked me to invite the heads of the clan to witness the formal transfer. I don't think he is trying to cheat me. He is a bit simpleminded, but he is honest. In some ways I would rather have a simpleminded man take custody of my business than someone who is sharp and calculating. I won't have to worry that my caretaker will scheme and cheat me out of my possessions. In any case, Master Wang is quite old. As far as I know he has no relatives. He would not have any heirs to will his wealth to even if he took over my possessions. Besides, I should outlive him. The wealth will come back to the Ma family some way or another."

Ma Wen-fui said, "Your plan sounds reasonable." Looking at Ma Liu and Ma Lung, he said, "What do you think?" Ma Liu said, "You know me, I do not like to meddle into decisions about handling business. Besides, I am the youngest member in this group. What does the eldest member of the clan say?" Ma Yü saw that although the three men were now receptive to his plans of temporary retirement, none of them wished to take the responsibility of being the first to voice consent. He slipped out of the study and brought back three bags. Laying them on the table, he opened the bags. When his three relatives saw the contents of the bags they were mesmerized. The bags contained priceless antiques. Ma Yü knew that his relatives did not lack money but that they all recognized a good piece of art when they saw one. The three men looked at the objects, then at each other, and nodded their heads.

Ma Liu said, "I think if our cousin wants to entrust his business to Master Wang temporarily, we should go along with his wishes. After all, he should be able to do what he wants with his possessions. If Uncle and Granduncle agree to witnessing the signing of the document with me, then I will see to it that the other relatives do not oppose it." Ma Wen-fui said immediately, "Ma Lung and I will gladly be witnesses along with you." Ma Lung nodded. "But," said Ma Wen-fui, "how are you going to get the other relatives to keep their peace on this matter?" Ma Liu whispered a few words into Ma Wen-fui's ear. Ma Wen-fui smiled broadly and said, "That is ingenious! Now we need not worry about dissenting factions in the clan!"

7

Ma Yü followed Sun Yüan-chen's plans and success-fully persuaded the leaders of the clan to endorse the transfer of his possessions to Wang Ch'ung-yang. The next day Ma Wen-fui asked Ma Liu to assemble the clan members and describe the situation to them. Ma Liu prepared his speech and addressed the clan: "Ma Yü wants to spend a few years in peace and quiet because of his weak health. He is transferring his possessions to Wang Ch'ung-yang so that someone trustworthy will take care it for the time being. Wang Ch'ung-yang will simply be a faithful watchdog over Ma Yü's possessions and no more." One relative said, "If that is the case, why not just appoint Wang Ch'ung-yang as custodian? What is the need for formal documents to seal the transfer?" Ma Liu replied, "You do not yet understand. Ma Yü is a careful man. He wants to be sure that Master Wang would treat his possessions with care and to assure this, Ma Yü must arrange to have Wang Ch'ung-yang formally 'possesses' his property and business. In this way, Wang Ch'ung-yang would guard Ma Yü's wealth as if it were his own." Another relative said, "If Wang Ch'ung-yang is the owner of Ma Yü's possessions, then Ma Yü will lose everything if Wang Ch'ung-yang runs away with them." Ma Liu said, "Wang Ch'ung-yang is an old man. He has no relatives. Where can he run to? Who would be his heirs? He is much older than Ma Yü. Certainly he will die before Ma Yü. Even if he is not willing to return Ma Yü's possessions once Ma Yu recovers from his illness, he will not live long to hold on to them. When he dies, the estate and business will return to Ma Yü. Do you understand now that Ma Yü is simply trying to get a faithful watchdog to take temporary care of his possessions?" The relatives nodded. Playing on the greed of the relatives, Ma Liu continued: "Listen, since Wang Ch'ung-yang is only a temporary watchdog and Ma Yü and his wife have no children, the estates and business will eventually go to our descendants. I think Wang Ch'ung-yang is an honest and virtuous man. Why not let Ma Yü appoint someone simpleminded and faithful to take care of his wealth temporarily?" The relatives fell in with Ma Liu's persuasive arguments and offered no more resistance to Ma Yü's plan of transferring his possessions to Wang Ch'ung-yang.

The next day the three clan leaders Ma Lung, Ma Wen-fui, and Ma Liu gathered at Ma Yü's mansion. That evening the clan members were invited for dinner, at which time the formal transfer of Ma Yü's possessions to Wang Ch'ung-yang was expected to be signed and witnessed. When the relatives arrived at the Ma mansion, they saw Ma Lung and Wang Ch'ung-yang sitting together drinking and talking as if they were the best of friends.

When all were seated for dinner, Ma Wen-fui stood up and addressed the clan. "Ma Yü wishes to transfer his possessions to Wang Ch'ung-yang. We are here tonight to witness and endorse the document of transfer. If there are any among you who disagree please do so now or hold your peace." This was merely a formality, as no opposition was expected after Ma Liu had swayed everyone into agreement the day before. After a brief period of silence, Ma Wen-fui asked Ma Yü to sign the document of transfer in front of the clan. Ma Liu, Ma Lung, and Ma Wen-fui then signed their signatures in endorsement. Three more clan elders signed as witnesses, and the transfer was formally sealed. Ma Yü took the document and handed it to Wang Ch'ung-yang. Dinner followed. Amidst the merriment Wang Ch'ung-yang was recognized formally as a "family member" of the Ma clan.

That evening, when the celebrations were over, Ma Yü said to his wife, "Thanks to your ingenious devices, we can now devote our lives to the cultivation of the Tao." Sun Yüan-chen said, "Let us wait a few days until our teacher is rested. Then we can approach him and go through the oath-taking ceremony that will make us his disciples."

Wang Ch'ung-yang had not been idle during this time, and now he began to plan a series of actions. He knew that although Ma Yü's relatives had been won over by Ma Liu's eloquence, he would now have to show that he was a trustworthy "watchdog." Immediately, he started a number of charitable projects. He

賄族長
馬鈺
立捨約
談玄
功重陽
傳真
修子桓

The leaders of the Ma clan are bribed. Ma Yü's wealth is transferred to Wang Ch'ung-yang.

38

provided for widows and orphans, paid off the debts of many impoverished farmers, made donations to local shrines, and provided subsidies to the county for public works such as bridges, roads, and irrigation ditches. People saw Wang Ch'ung-yang's activities and praised him for his virtuous deeds. The Ma clan also received compliments for having selected a wise and virtuous custodian. Thus no words of discontent arose from the clan members.

While Wang Ch'ung-yang was designing charitable projects, he was also building facilities in the Ma mansion for a retreat. In a remote area of the Ma mansion, meditation huts, dormitories, and an instruction hall were being erected. On the appointed day, Ma Yü and Sun Yüan-chen approached Wang Ch'ung-yang and formally became his disciples. Wang Ch'ung-yang told them, "The Taoist path is a path of awakening and knowing. Those who walk it will return to the truth. Entrance to the path should be gradual. Your training should follow a sequence, starting from the easy and graduating to the difficult. Those who aspire to cultivate the Tao must first find their original nature. Original nature is the original state of things, or "Earlier Heaven." You must cultivate your original nature until it is smooth and bright. If original nature is not cultivated, feelings will be wild. Untamed feelings are like tigers and dragons. If you cannot tame these animals in you, how can you become one with the void? The Tao is without form. You must dissolve your ego, for the ego is the source of form and attachment. You must learn how to subdue the tiger and the dragon and tame the monkey and the wild horse. A wild intelligence is like a monkey. It plays tricks on you and makes you mistake the impermanent for the real. Egotistic intentions are like wild horses. They drag you away from the purity and stillness of original nature. If you do not tame the wild horse and the mischievous monkey, then you will not understand the mysteries of heaven and earth, the balance of *yin* and *yang*, and the power of silence in moving the universe. The clockwise path is mortality; the counterclockwise path is immortality. To empty the heart of desire and thoughts, to be in the void, is to emerge with the Tao. The Tao cannot be grasped by thoughts. It must be experienced directly with the heart. When you have made progress I shall instruct you further in these matters."

Ma Yü and Sun Yüan-chen thanked Wang Chung-yang for initiating them into the Tao. They each took a Taoist name. Ma Yü was named Ma Tan-yang, meaning "bright *yang*," and Sun Yüan-chen was named Sun Pu-erh, meaning "one-hearted." Returning to their bedroom, Sun Pu-erh said to Ma Tan-yang, "Before initiation into the Tao we were husband and wife and shared a room. After initiation we are brother and sister in the Tao. From now on, I shall address you as "brother" and you will call me "friend in the Tao." We shall stay in separate rooms so we can devote ourselves singularly to our training." Ma Tan-yang said, "If not for you I would never have been able to come this far. I shall honor you as 'friend in the Tao,' and we shall stay in separate rooms." Ma Tan-yang then ordered a servant to clean out a guest room and stayed there, far from the bedroom of his wife.

Half a month passed, and Sun Pu-erh sent a servant with a message to Ma Tan-yang. They met at the door of Wang Ch'ung-yang's room, for they wanted to ask the teacher about the original state of things. Wang Ch'ung-yang received them and they asked, "Teacher, you mentioned that original nature is part of the original state of things, called Earlier Heaven. What is Earlier Heaven like? Can you describe it to us?" Wang Ch'ung-yang replied, "Earlier Heaven is the original breath. It has no form or structure. Therefore it cannot be described. That which can be pointed to and described is not Earlier Heaven. When the heart is not empty of thoughts, forms arise and Earlier Heaven is lost. Earlier Heaven is not here or there, or this or that. Look for it, and it disappears."

8

When Ch'ung-yang said, "I shall explain original nature to you with a picture. However, understand that original nature cannot be conceptualized or described. My drawing is therefore only an approximation." Taking a brush, he dipped it into some ink and drew a circle on a piece of paper. Inside the circle he drew a dot. Then he said to Ma Tan-yang and Sun Pu-erh, "Do you know what this represents?" They replied, "Sir, we do not know. Instruct us." Wang Ch'ung-yang said, "The circle represents the undifferentiated whole, a state of existence before heaven and earth emerged. This state is called *Wu-chi*. From *Wu-chi*, *T'ai-chi* is born. This is the dot in the circle. From *T'ai-chi*, everything in the universe is born. The life-giving breath of *T'ai-chi* is the one breath of Earlier Heaven. From the one breath of Earlier Heaven emerges original nature. Original nature was there before we were born. It will be there after we die. Original nature is also called the knowing spirit. It is not born, and it never dies. Everyone has original nature. We do not see it because it is often clouded by craving, desire, and evil thoughts. If we do not sweep away that which hides our original nature, we will lose our connection with Earlier Heaven and be doomed to countless lifetimes of suffering. How does one reconnect with Earlier Heaven? Earlier Heaven must be experienced with the heart of the Tao. If one tries to understand Earlier Heaven with the ego, one will never find it. Earlier Heaven and original nature are in front of us. We cannot see it because the ego has constructed a barrier. If we are able to dissolve the ego, then original nature, or the heart of the Tao, will emerge. When the heart of the Tao emerges, Earlier Heaven will appear. How does one cultivate the heart of the Tao and dissolve the egotistic heart? When a person is ill, simply getting rid of the symptom will not ensure that the illness will never return. The cause of the illness must be eradicated. Similarly, we must find the root of the barriers which separate us from Earlier Heaven. The ancient sages and immortals have understood these causes and have set down guidelines for eradicating them. I shall transmit their teachings to you.

"If you want to get rid of the sickness of spirit and body, you must get to its cause. If you know the cause, then you will know the cure. The primary cause of ill health is none other than craving. Craving creates the obstacles to health. These obstacles are desire for liquor, sexual desire, greed for riches, and bad temper. Those who wish to cultivate health and longevity must first remove these obstacles. Sever all attachment to external things and dissolve desires. Then the internal illness will disappear and the root of ill health will be eradicated. Once health is regained, the cultivation of the Tao and the attainment of immortality are possible.

"First, let us discuss the obstacle of liquor. Many people know that liquor can disrupt reason and therefore want to abstain from it. Others abstain because they are persuaded to do so by friends and relatives. Yet others abstain because the law forbids it. However, when they see liquor or when they see others drink, they desire it. Even if no liquor has touched their lips, the very craving shows that they have not overcome the obstacle. Craving originates in thoughts. Even before the thought becomes action, craving already exists and the damage has been done. Getting rid of the obstacle of liquor requires the absence of craving in thought as well as in action.

"Now, take sexual desire. Many people know that sexual desire drains the generative energy and want to abstain from it. However, when they see an attractive person they fantasize about having sex or secretly desire sexual company. When these thoughts arise, even if one is not engaged in sex physically, one is already prey to the obstacle. You now understand that the cause of craving after liquor and sex lies in the mind. If you want to remove these obstacles, you must start with eradicating the thoughts of desire from your mind. Tame the heart [mind], and the intentions will not run wild. When the heart is emptied of desire, the cause of ill health will disappear. Cut the attachments externally, and the internal injuries will be healed. Your heart should be clear and calm like a still lake reflecting the light of

談先天真
一妙理
除魔根不
二法門
子桓

Wang Ch'ung-yang expounds the one true reality.

43

the moon. If ripples appear on the water, then the image of the moon will be distorted and the Tao will never be realized in you.

"How does one go about eradicating the desire for liquor and sex? The ancient sages offer this advice: If it is not proprietous, do not look at it. If it is not proprietous, do not do it. If it is in front of you, behave as if you saw nothing. If it is spoken to you, behave as if you heard nothing. The Buddhists teach: "Forget the other, forget oneself, forget everyone." The Taoists teach: "Look but do not see it; hear but do not listen." [That is, if you are not attached to the liquor or the sexual attraction, those things will lose their attractiveness. Attraction is not in the object itself but in the attitude that we carry around with us.] If you can do this, then you will have eradicated the desire for liquor and sex.

"As for riches, this is a difficult obstacle to overcome. There are those who are poor and need to work hard to earn a living for themselves and their family. Therefore, they do not have much choice but to focus their attention on acquiring money. People in this condition must live with their karma and wait for another lifetime to relinquish their ties with money. Then there are those who crave riches so that they may display their wealth and earn the respect and admiration of others. Yet further there are those who crave riches for a life of luxury and waste. And then there are those who accumulate riches because they wish to exploit misfortune and see others suffer. It is these latter kinds of craving for riches that prevent one from discovery of the Tao.

"Temper is the result of emotions running wild. There are positive and negative feelings. Positive feelings like compassion, empathy, and humility are to be cultivated, but negative feelings such as anger, bad temper, and cruelty should be dissolved. Bad temper is the result of self-importance. Bad temper is harmful to health because it creates bad *ch'i* in our bodies. Verbal arguments, competitiveness, aggressiveness, impatience, frustration, annoyance are all manifestations of bad temper. How can people with these dispositions attain the Tao?

"If you wish to eradicate the bad temper and the desire for riches, listen to the sages. They give good advice. The Confucianists say, 'Riches that do not rightfully belong to me I see as

44

empty as the floating clouds. Take control of your reason, and you will not lose your temper.' The Buddhists say, 'Do not crave rewards. Virtue comes from the ability to resist provocation.' The Taoists say, 'Know the illusion of material goods. Cultivate compassion, and your temper will be calmed.' Take these words of advice and you will be able to eradicate bad temper and desire for riches.

"To eradicate the four obstacles to health—liquor, sexual desire, riches, and bad temper—one must cultivate the heart. Once the heart is tamed, the cause of ill health will disappear. The Confucianists tell us to 'awaken.' The Buddhists tell us to 'understand.' The Taoists tell us to 'act intuitively.' First, we need to *awaken* to the fact that we have fallen prey to the obstacles. Second, we need to *understand* what the obstacles are and their causes. Lastly, we need to *act intuitively*, that is, to act spontaneously from a heart that is tamed of desire and craving. If you can do these things, then you will have no problem attaining the Tao."

Ma Tan-yang and Sun Pu-erh asked about meditation. Wang Ch'ung-yang said, "In meditation all thoughts must cease. When the ego is dead, the spirit emerges. When you sit, sit on a cushion. Loosen your clothing. At the hour of *tzu* (11:00 P.M.), cross your legs gently and sit facing east. Clasp your hands together and place them in front of your body. Your back should be straight. Strike your teeth together and swallow your saliva. Place the tongue against the palate of your mouth. You should be alert in listening, but do not be attached to sounds. Let your eyes drop, but do not close them. Focus on the light that you see in front of you and concentrate on the Lower *t'an-t'ien*. In meditation it is very important to stop thinking. If thoughts arise, the spirit will not be pure, and your efforts of cultivation will come to nothing. In addition, you should drop all feelings. Once feelings arise, the heart will not be still, and the attainment of the Tao is impossible."

Wang Ch'ung-yang continued, "Sit on a cushion and you will be able to sit long and not feel tired. Loosen your clothing so the movement of internal energy will not be constricted. The hour of *tzu* is when the first ray of *yang* appears. Face east because the breath of life flows in from the east at the hour of first *yang*. Clasp your hands in the *t'ai-chi* symbol, because it symbolizes emptiness of form. Sit with your back straight, because only with a vertical spine can the energy rise to the head. Close your mouth and place the tongue against the palate so that the internal energy cannot dissipate. The ear is associated with generative energy. Being attached to sound will dissipate this energy. Do not close your eyes, for they let the light in to shine on your spirit. If you close your eyes, the spirit will be dimmed. If you open them too wide, the spirit will escape. Therefore you should lower the lids but not close them. Concentrate on the Lower *t'an-t'ien* as if to reflect the light of your eyes on it because here is the mystery of all things. Minimize speech, as this conserves vital energy. Rest your ears, as this conserves generative energy. Dissolve thoughts to conserve spiritual energy. When all these energies are not dissipated, then you will attain immortality."

Ma Tan-yang and Sun Pu-erh thanked Wang Ch'ung-yang for his instructions. Wang Ch'ung-yang added, "Staying on the path of the Tao requires discipline. You should take this knowledge seriously and practice it all the time. Otherwise, even though you know what to do, you will accomplish nothing." Ma Tan-yang and Sun Pu-erh bowed and left. They returned to their rooms and began to meditate according to Wang Ch'ung-yang's instructions. A few months passed in this way, and they began to experience changes in their bodies. Thinking that they had now grasped all the teachings of the Tao, they stopped visiting Wang Ch'ung-yang for further instruction.

One day Ma Tan-yang was meditating in his room and saw Wang Ch'ung-yang enter. Ma Tan-yang stood up to welcome his teacher. Wang Ch'ung-yang said, "The Tao is limitless. It can be used continuously and yet never dry up. It is flexible and can cloak itself in countless shapes. Do not hold on to one of its many manifestations. Be sincere and humble in your learning. Only then will your body benefit from your training."

Wang Ch'ung-yang continued to teach Ma Tan-yang. "If your heart is not true, you cannot cultivate the Tao. Every action and every thought must come from a true heart. If your heart is sick, then it must be healed. Tame the selfish heart with a selfless heart. Tame the desirous heart with a heart of reason. Tame the heart of extreme tendencies with moderation. Tame the proud heart with a humble heart. Find where the problems are and counter each of them. If you are able to do this, then the problems will never arise. Your heart will be like the spring wind. Your mind will be bright as the moon in a clear sky. Your heart will be open like the wide plains, and your being will be as still and rooted as the mountains. The internal energy will circulate through your body. Without realizing it, you will have attained the Tao."

While Wang Ch'ung-yang was discussing Taoist internal alchemy with Ma Tan-yang, Sun Pu-erh was meditating in her room. She heard a sound and saw Wang Ch'ung-yang enter. Shocked and frightened, she stood up. Before she could say anything, Wang Ch'ung-yang said, "The way of the Tao is intricate and mysterious. Although there are many methods, there is only one truth. The teachings of all sects draw from the origin. One must not be rigid. Practice naturally, and you will achieve effects. You have been sitting here all alone, thinking that there is only one way to cultivate the Tao. Do you know that *yin* cannot flourish without *yang?* Simply sitting will not balance the *yin* and *yang* in your body. If your *yin* and *yang* do not copulate, how can you become pregnant and give birth to a child? You don't understand this and you don't understand that. How can you cultivate the Tao?" Sun Pu-erh was beginning to get annoyed. Wang Ch'ung-yang's words sounded like gibberish to her. Moreover, she felt intruded upon and insulted. Without a word Sun Pu-erh ran out of her room and ordered a servant to fetch her husband. The servant ran to Ma Tan-yang and said, "Master, the lady is very upset and angry and wants to talk to you at once." All this time, Ma Tan-yang was sitting in his room conversing with Wang Ch'ung-yang. Respectfully he took leave of his teacher and followed the servant, to find Sun Pu-erh fretting and pouting in the living room.

9

$\mathcal{O}n$ $finding$ his wife in a sour mood, Ma Tan-yang said to her good-naturedly, "What is the problem? Is it because the servants were not doing their duties? If so, forgive them. We as Taoists should not be upset over such things." Sun Pu-erh said, "Brother, you do not know. We thought that Wang Ch'ung-yang was an enlightened teacher, and we were wrong. That old man had the gall to enter my bedroom without my consent and started speaking nonsense. We should stop studying with him. He is not an upright man." Ma Tan-yang was puzzled. "This is strange. You said Wang Ch'ung-yang was in your room a while ago. Yet all morning he was with me in my room, and he was there when you sent for me." Before Sun Pu-erh could reply, the servant said, "Yes, when I went to fetch the master, I saw Mr. Wang sitting in the master's room." Sun Pu-erh was confused. Ma Tan-yang shook his head and walked back to his room. Sun Pu-erh was becoming frustrated. She had thought that if she complained to Ma Tan-yang about Wang Ch'ung-yang's behavior she would vent her anger and Wang Ch'ung-yang would at least be rebuked for his shameless actions. On the contrary, she was being silenced. She stamped back to her room and closed the door.

A month had passed, when Wang Ch'ung-yang appeared at Ma Tan-yang's room again. He sat down, sighed, and said, "People think that cultivating the Tao is nothing but attending to their daily speech, how they should dress, what they should hear, and what they should eat. They do not know that they are trying to mold the Tao according to their conception of what it is. Thus they have lost the essence of the Tao. And then there are others who look for secretive methods and thereby stray into evil paths, and those who have the right intention but are weak in will. And there are those who worry too much about their progress. They advance an inch, but their anxiety sets them back ten feet. The Tao cannot be grasped with the ego. As long as the ego exists, the heart of the Tao cannot emerge. If one cannot cut the ties to gain and loss and to social pressures; if one is concerned with whether one's appearance is appealing, whether one's food is the best, whether one's wealth is acknowledged, and whether one's property is large, then one has not learned to see through the illusions of material things. Craving breeds anxiety. If you crave, then you will be anxious to obtain what you desire. Once you have it, you will fear that it may be lost. If you do not get what you desire, you will be disappointed. The ego is the source of craving. If you want to dissolve it, you must cut your ties to gain and loss. All persons possess the original nature of Earlier Heaven, which has the potential of attaining the Tao. They fail because they are unable to overcome the dominance of the ego. Ego causes attachment, but the heart of the Tao is not attched to anything. It is not attached to beauty, ugliness, gains, losses, destruction, fame, fortune, even life or death. The heart of Tao is capable of cutting through illusions and hindrances to the attainment of immortality. Awaken the heart of the Tao in yourself, and your effort of cultivation will bear fruit."

While Wang Ch'ung-yang was explaining the importance of dissolving the ego and cutting ties to gains and losses to Ma Tan-yang, Sun Pu-erh was sitting in her room still confused and annoyed over Wang Ch'ung-yang's unannounced visit one month earlier. As she was dozing off to sleep she heard a noise, and opening her eyes she saw Wang Ch'ung-yang standing by the doorway. He smiled, walked in, and said, "Know that in the Tao there is no division of male and female. If you separate *yin* and *yang* the Tao cannot be attained." Sun Pu-erh invited him to sit down and stood by his side near the door. Apprehensively, she asked, "Sir, you usually spend your time meditating in your room. What is the purpose of your visit?" Wang Ch'ung-yang said, "I came because I see that you are in peril. You have distanced yourself from the True Stove. Your training has been unbalanced. Your "dead" sitting has made you irritable and inflexible. Know that male and female cannot exist without each other. *Yin* and *yang* must copulate. The Yellow Woman must act as the go-between so that the pair can unite. When male and female are united, the fetus can be conceived. After ten months of pregnancy, the child can be born. If you follow my instructions you will ascend to the heavens and meet the Jade Emperor." Sun

王重陽分

身化度

孫不二念

怒肓師

子桓 〔印〕

*Wang Ch'ung-yang's spirit visits Sun Pu-erh. Sun Pu-erh is
annoyed at her teacher's behavior.*

Pu-erh quickly slipped out of the room and locked the door behind her. She ran to Ma Tan-yang's room and found no one there. The servants informed her that Ma Tan-yang was at the meditation hall receiving instructions from Master Wang. Sun Pu-erh went there at once.

All this time Wang Ch'ung-yang had been with Ma Tan-yang, instructing him how to overcome the barriers that can prevent one from attaining the Tao. They were deep in conversation when Wang Ch'ung-yang said, "Someone is looking for you. You had better go outside and see who it is." Ma Tan-yang ran into Sun Pu-erh right in front of the meditation hall. Sun Pu-erh grabbed Ma Tan-yang's sleeves and said, "Come and look." Ma Tan-yang said, "What do you want me to look at?" Sun Pu-erh replied, "When we get there you'll understand." She pulled him to her room, where she thought she had Wang Ch'ung-yang locked inside. Opening the lock, she said, "Now please go in and look." Ma Tan-yang did not know what his wife was up to, but he went into the room nonetheless. He looked around and returned to Sun Pu-erh, saying, "I see nothing unusual. What is the matter?" Sun Pu-erh replied, "Did you see Master Wang?" Ma Tan-yang said, "There is no one in your room. Besides, he has been with me all day." Sun Pu-erh could not believe it. She went inside the room, looked in the closets, under the bed, and behind the curtains. "I definitely locked Wang Ch'ung-yang inside. How come he's not in here? This is strange." Ma Tan-yang said, "There is nothing strange about all this. Your heart was not clear, and you fell to the prey of the monsters of illusion." Sun Pu-erh said, "I do not understand. I thought I was disciplined and focused in my training. How could I have strayed and hallucinated? When Master Wang was here talking to me, he was very real, I still remember clearly everything he said. I do not think I was hallucinating or dreaming those incidents." Ma Tan-yang said, "Tell me what he said to you." Sun Pu-erh related everything Wang Ch'ung-yang had said.

When Sun Pu-erh had finished, Ma Tan-yang laughed and said, "You have always been smart, but this time you missed." Sun Pu-erh asked, "Where did I miss?" Ma Tan-yang replied, "Those who seek the Tao must be humble and patient and willing to learn. Otherwise you will not progress. The Tao is limitless. If you think you have learned everything about it, you have lost it. You were sitting in your room doing what you were instructed to do a long time ago. You thought that by gaining some progress you had completely mastered the methods of internal alchemy. Master Wang saw that you were stagnating to the point of losing what you have achieved. That was why he came to instruct you. His spirit left his body and came to your room. That was how he could be with you and me at the same time."

Ma Tan-yang continued, "By the union of male and female, Master Wang did not mean the physical relationship between man and woman. He was referring to the *yin* and *yang* energies in our body. If the two energies are isolated, your training will be unbalanced: you will have either too much *yang* or too much *yin*. *Yang* is fire in nature. Too much fire, and you will burn the herbs. *Yin* is water in nature. Too much water, and the herbs will rot. Either way, the Golden Pill cannot materialize. *Yang* is the clear, conceptualizing intelligence; *yin* is the receptive, intuiting quietude. You have had too much *yang* in your training. You were analyzing too much at the expense of intuition. The Yellow Woman is the true intention that can bring together the opposites and unite the *yin* and *yang*. Yellow is the color of the element earth. It occupies the central position and belongs to the element wood. *Yin* occupies the western position and belongs to the element metal. Without the Yellow Woman, metal will destroy wood as an axe cuts a tree. *Yin* and *yang* will be in opposition rather than act as complementary pairs. When wood and metal are joined, this is the union of male and female. The union takes place in the cauldron where the three herbs are gathered and sealed. The herbs are none other than your internal energy in its three forms: generative, vital, and spiritual energy. In this union, your soul and spirit are merged. This is what is referred to as the merging of lead and mercury. Out of this union, a fetus is conceived. This fetus is the spirit. Ten is a number of completeness. When the fetus has been nourished for a sufficient time, the spirit will leave the body at an opening in the crown of the head. It will ascend to the heavens and become an immortal in the realm of the Jade Emperor." When Ma Tan-yang finished speaking, Sun Pu-erh said, "Brother, now I understand."

10

Sun Pu=erh felt as if she had awakened from a bad dream. Everything now seemed clear. She sighed and said to Ma Tan-yang, "Brother, if not for your help I would have remained in the depths of illusion and ruined myself. Usually I am more intelligent in dealing with daily matters, but when it comes to learning Taoist knowledge you surpass me by far." Ma Tan-yang said, "It is not because I grasp the instructions of our teacher better, but because for a long time you closed your mind to learning new things. You thought you had learned all there was to learn. Your intelligence became an obstacle to your training. Learning is limitless. Not many can fully grasp this idea." Sun Pu-erh thanked Ma Tan-yang and said, "From now on I shall be humble and learn whatever there is to learn." Ma Tan-yang returned to his room, happy that Sun Pu-erh had realized her mistakes and was now ready to progress again.

A few days later Ma Tan-yang prepared to attend the birthday celebration of an aunt in a nearby town. He asked Sun Pu-erh to accompany him, but she pleaded sick and said she could not make the journey. So Ma Tan-yang packed the gifts, loaded them on a mule, and set out alone.

Sun Pu-erh sat in her room and thought once more about Ma Tan-yang's words. She especially remembered his saying that she had lost her motivation to learn. Left alone in the mansion, she thought things through. Ma Tan-yang would be away for a few days, and the servants were busy. This would be a good opportunity for her to go to Wang Ch'ung-yang and humbly ask for instructions.

She went to the meditation hall and found Wang Ch'ung-yang sitting quietly in meditation. She knelt at the doorway and said respectfully, "Sir, your student Sun Pu-erh has been stupid and did not appreciate your teachings. Now that Ma Tan-yang has explained everything to me, I am ashamed of myself and what I have done. I would like to ask for forgiveness and hope that you will instruct me again." She bowed low several times. Wang

Ch'ung-yang beckoned her in and said, "You may stand up now. I shall describe to you three vehicles of the Taoist path. Listen well and then tell me which vehicle you aspire toward. Those who seek that Tao are nonattached to life and death. The heart is void of form and free from dust. There are no thoughts or feelings that tie one to the material plane. Their being is like the bright moon in a cloudless sky. With the spark of original nature they intuit the mystery of heaven and earth. They understand the principles behind the union of *yin* and *yang,* and, using the methods of internal alchemy, they return to the void and emerge with the Tao. They are at one with the sun and moon, they age with the heaven and earth and achieve the highest rank of immortality in heaven. This is the Great Vehicle. It is the fastest and the most direct path to immortality. Those who cultivate the Middle Vehicle observe the festivals of the gods and immortals with veneration, chant regularly the names of the gods and refrain from meat on designated vegetarian days. By immersing themselves in chanting, they purify the heart and let the original nature shine. In due time their spirit ascends to the heavens, and they become immortals of the middle rank. Those who cultivate the Lower Vehicle do good deeds, and by so doing their original nature is prevented from being tainted. They are contented and are at peace with themselves, living a long and healthy life. In due time, when they have accumulated enough good works, they will ascend to heaven and become immortals of the lower ranks."

Wang Ch'ung-yang finished speaking, smiled, and asked Sun Pu-erh, "To which vehicle do you aspire?" Sun Pu-erh replied, "Your student aspires to the Great Vehicle." Wang Ch'ung-yang said, "You have ambitions aspirations, but I don't know whether you have the discipline and perseverance to pursue that path." Sun Pu-erh said, "Sir, my aspirations are not ambitious, but my will is strong. I am willing to sacrifice everything to attain the Great Vehicle."

Wang Ch'ung-yang then said, "Those who cultivate the Tao must find a place that is conducive to training. Certain places are filled with power, and training at these power places will enhance one's progress. There is a power hidden in the city of Loyang, and the gods have ordained that an immortal will emerge from

Wang Ch'ung-yang expounds the three levels of the cultivation of the Tao. Sun Pu-erh resolves to go to Loyang and disfigures her face with hot oil.

there. One need merely cultivate oneself there for ten to twelve years, and immortality will be attained. Are you willing to go?" Sun Pu-erth said, "I am willing to go anywhere if that is what is required to cultivate the Great Vehicle." Wang Ch'ung-yang looked at Sun Pu-erh and then shook his head. "You cannot go." Sun Pu-erh said, "I am willing to do anything. I am willing to die, if necessary." Wang Ch'ung-yang said, "Dying is a waste if it achieves no purpose. To simply throw your life away is to rob yourself of the chance to become an immortal. Loyang is more than a thousand miles away. You will meet with perils along the way. You will be the target of men who desire your beauty. They will rape you and molest you. And rather than be shamed, you would take your own life before they touch you. Now, is that not wasting your life to no purpose? Not only will you not achieve immortality but you will throw away what was given to you by Heaven. That is why I said you cannot go."

Sun Pu-erh left the meditation hall and went directly to the kitchen. Telling the servants to leave, she filled a wok with cooking oil, heated the oil until it was hot, and then poured in cold water. The oil sizzled, and sparks of hot liquid shot out of the wok. Sun Pu-erh closed her eyes and let the liquid hit her face, burning the skin in numerous places; even after healing, the burns would leave scars and marks all over her face. She then returned to Wang Ch'ung-yang and said, "Look at my ugly face. Now will you allow me to travel to Loyang?" Wang Ch'ung-yang clapped his hands and said, "I have never seen one as determined as you are or willing to sacrifice so much. I did not come to Shantung Province in vain. You shall go to Loyang."

Wang Ch'ung-yang then taught Sun Pu-erh the methods of internal alchemy. He showed her how to immerse fire in water, how to unite *yin* and *yang*, and how to conceive and nourish the spirit. When he was satisfied that Sun Pu-erh remembered and understood the instructions, he said, "Remember, hide your knowledge. Do not let people know you are a seeker of the Tao. After you have finished the Great Alchemical Work, then you may reveal yourself and teach others. In the meantime, let your face heal. Do not even let your servants know of your plans. Leave as soon as you are ready. You need not come to say farewell to me. We shall meet again soon at the celebration of the ripening of the immortal peach."

Sun Pu-erh thanked Wang Ch'ung-yang and left the meditation hall. On her way back to her room, she ran into a servant, who screamed when she saw the lady's face. When the servant recovered her wits, she asked Sun Pu-erh, "Lady, what has happened to your face?" Sun Pu-erh said, "I was cooking a snack for the teacher, and by mistake I added water to the cooking oil. I did not get out of the way in time, and the sizzling liquid shot into my face. It is nothing serious." Sun Pu-erh locked herself in her room for the next few days and reviewed Wang Ch'ung-yang's instructions.

When Ma Tan-yang returned home, the servants at once told him about his wife's accident in the kitchen. Ma Tan-yang went to Sun Pu-erh's room, saw her face, and consoled her. Gently he said, "You should have been more careful. Let the servants do the cooking. The lady of the house should not be working in the kitchen. Now your beautiful face is ruined with scars." Sun Pu-erh stared at Ma Tan-yang and cackled madly. "Are you the messenger of the Empress of Heaven? Have you come to invite me to attend the celebrations in heaven? If so, let's get going!" She opened the window and jumped out. Pretending to slip, she deliberately fell and lay on the ground, groaning. Ma Tan-yang ran out, put his arms around her and helped her up. Sun Pu-erh laughed and cried like a mad woman. Ma Tan-yang escorted her back to her room and then went to Wang Ch'ung-yang.

Seeing his teacher, Ma Tan-yang said, "Sir, my wife has gone mad. She has lost her mind. She is talking nonsense, and she laughs and cries for no reason." Wang Ch'ung-yang said, "If she is not mad, how can she become an immortal?" Ma Tan-yang did not understand Wang Ch'ung-yang's remark. He was about to ask his teacher what it meant when Wang Ch'ung-yang waved his hand and told him to leave. Sadly, Ma Tan-yang went back to his room.

Sun Pu-erh's pretended insanity succeeded in getting Ma Tan-yang and everyone else in the mansion to leave her alone. She reviewed Wang Ch'ung-yang's instructions repeatedly until she could perform them naturally and effortlessly. A month passed, and Sun Pu-erh looked at her face in the mirror. Scars and pockmarks dotted her face. Since she had not combed her hair for a month, she was no longer the beautiful wife of a wealthy merchant. Sun Pu-erh was delighted. She was now ready to make the journey to Loyang. With a piece of charcoal she smeared her face and her clothing. Looking like a mad beggar-woman, she ran out into the living room, laughed wildly, and rushed out the front door. A servant tried to stop her, but she bit the girl in the arm. Yelping in pain, the servant let go of her. The other servants alerted Ma Tan-yang. He hurried to the living room, but was told that the lady had already left the house. Ma Tan-yang and the servants searched the town and the immediate countryside for Sun Pu-erh, but they could not find her.

Knowing that Ma Tan-yang would search for her, Sun Pu-erh had hidden herself inside a haystack on a nearby farm. She heard the voices of the servants and her husband and continued to conceal herself until it was dark. When everything was silent, she quietly slipped out and walked toward Loyang. Along the way, she slept in abandoned temples and caves. She obtained her food from begging, and when people asked who she was, she acted insane and uttered nonsense. In this way, people left her alone, and eventually she arrived safely at Loyang.

11

In Loyang, Sun Pu-erh found shelter in an abandoned house. Daily she begged in the city. When people tried to communicate with her, she acted insane, and as time went on she became known as the "mad beggar-woman." Because of her ugly face and her madness, the townspeople left her alone and she was able to practice internal alchemy without distraction.

In the city of Loyang there were two wanderers of seedy character called Chang San and Li Ssu. They solicited every woman they saw, and they raped those who refused their company. One day the two men saw Sun Pu-erh begging on a street corner. They noticed that despite her rags and the scars on her face Sun Pu-erh was quite attractive. That night, when Chang San and Li Ssu were returning home from an evening at the brothels, it occurred to Chang San that they might finish their evening of fun with the mad beggar-woman. When he voiced his plan to Li Ssu, the latter said, "We cannot do that. Don't you know the saying 'Those who take advantage of mad people will meet with bad luck all their lives'?" Chang San said, "I don't care about the superstitious sayings of old women. I am not afraid of the gods of Heaven or earth. I am going to have some fun with that woman." Chang San strode ahead toward the abandoned house where Sun Pu-erh was living. Li Ssu followed behind apprehensively.

Just as the abandoned house came into view, ominous storm clouds gathered in the sky. Suddenly there was a flash of lightning and a loud crack of thunder. When Chang San and Li Ssu recovered from the deafening sound, they found that they were being struck by enormous hailstones. Since they were on the outskirts of town, they had to run a good distance before they could find shelter from the balls of ice. As they ran, Li Ssu said to his friend, "You should have listened to me. That was the wrath of Heaven coming down on us." Chang San cursed under his breath and tried to run faster, but he tripped over a pile of logs hidden by the tall grass and fell into a thorny bush. Bruised and bleeding, he got up and staggered toward the gates of the inner city.

By the time Chang San and Li Ssu reached the inner city, the sky had cleared and a bright moon shone. Chang San was bleeding badly. He had been pelted by enormous hailstones and cut by sharp thorns. Li Ssu, on the contrary, had not received a single scratch. It appeared that only the small hailstones had struck him. Chang San finally sighed and said, "I am convinced. That mad woman cannot be touched." Li Ssu replied, "Now you know. I hope that you have learned your lesson well this time and will not try to bother her again." Chang San said, "The lesson was learned well. From now on I will not even walk in the direction of that abandoned house."

The next day Li Ssu related the incident to all his friends, and the story spread around the city. From then on in the town no one made fun of her when she begged or went near the abandoned house she was living in. Thus Sun Pu-erh was left in peace for the twelve years that she lived in Loyang.

Back in Shantung Province, after Sun Pu-erh's mysterious disappearance, tongues began to wag. One man said, "Master Ma is so stupid. He gave all his wealth to this fellow Wang Ch'ung-yang, who squandered so much of it by giving it away. And do you know, his pretty wife became insane because she could not stand what was going on. Now she has run off and probably drowned herself in some river." Another man, called Chia Jen-an, said, "The Ma mansion has become utterly strange. I went there yesterday to visit Master Ma. There were no servants at the door, so I went directly into the living room. The place looked deserted. In the past there were always plenty of people coming and going. But now, it looks like an abandoned house. I saw a servant and asked to see the master. The servant told me that Master Ma was in the meditation hall in the back garden. There I found Master Ma sitting quietly inside a thatched hut. When he noticed me, he came out and greeted me. I asked him if he had any information regarding his wife's whereabouts. He replied that she had her own path and he had his. I then asked what had become of his large household, and he said that he had given his younger servants some money and told them to start a

降水雹天
公護法
施妙算真
人指迷
長沙郝子桓

The vagabonds are struck by a hailstorm. Sun Pu-erh
meditates in peace in an abandoned dwelling.

life of their own. When I asked about the thatched huts in the back garden, he told me that they were built to accommodate seekers of the Tao. Finally I gave up and left. On my way out I saw an old servant and asked him why the place had suddenly changed from a busy household to this quiet, almost monastery-like atmosphere. The old servant replied that both Wang Ch'ung-yang and Ma Tan-yang liked to live a simple and undisturbed life far from the dust of the daily world. He also said that Wang Ch'ung-yang is an immortal who can see into the future, that he can read people's minds and can predict what they will do, and that he can even tell when it will rain."

After Chia Jen-an had told a captive audience about the strange goings-on in the Ma mansion, an elderly man with the family name of Pan said, "If this Wang Ch'ung-yang can really see into the future, then let us go ask him when it will rain. It has been a long time since it rained. If we know when the next rains will come, then we can make plans as to whether we should harvest our crops now or wait for the next rains." The crowd thought this was a good idea, and presently a large group of people gathered at the Ma mansion. Ma Tan-yang received them, and when the old man Pan had voiced his query he went and asked Wang Ch'ung-yang, "Sir, the villagers would like to know when the next rains will come." Wang Ch'ung-yang replied, "Tell them to go to the Earth God temple in the eastern section of town. On the wall they will see that date on which the rains will come." Ma Tan-yang relayed the information to the villagers.

The villagers went to the temple and found on a shadowed wall a row of faint characters. Someone lit a torch, and the old man Pan read them aloud: "The Wang family will be crowned with pearls. On the twenty-third day of the month it will rain. The mouth of the monk is filled with mud." The old man turned to the crowd and said, "These are just words strung together nonsensically. There is no logic in the context." Chia Jen-an spoke out from the crowd, "Did you note the second phrase? It clearly says that it will rain on the twenty-third day." Old man Pan said, "That was a coincidence. Besides, the phrase is embedded in a context which is utterly nonsensical. I am afraid you are all fooled by this self-proclaimed immortal, Wang Ch'ung-yang."

Chia Jen-an was not about to be convinced. Addressing the villagers, he said, "Look, today is the nineteenth day of the month. The words said that it will rain on the twenty-third. We need not argue. Let us wait for the twenty-third before we decide whether Wang Ch'ung-yang is a fraud or not. After all, we need only wait four days to find out." The villagers murmured approval and went back to their homes.

On the morning of the twenty-third day the skies were dark with rain clouds. Suddenly the rains came down and did not stop until late afternoon. After that Wang Ch'ung-yang was recognized without dispute as an immortal who could see into the future.

A few days later, a villager from the northern section of town who had lost a water buffalo came to Wang Ch'ung-yang for help. Wang Ch'ung-yang said, "Go to the tallest tree in the southern section of town. Climb to the top of the tree where the birds build their nests, and you will find the water buffalo." The man laughed and said, "Master, surely you joke. How can a water buffalo climb up to the top of a tree?" Wang Ch'ung-yang simply replied, "If you want your buffalo, climb the tree." The man left and decided there would be no harm in climbing the tree. At least he would be satisfied that it was not there.

The villager found the tallest tree in the southern section of town and climbed to the top. There he had an unobstructed view of the town. Remembering Wang Ch'ung-yang's words, he looked toward a branch where a bird's nest was perched and he saw his water buffalo chained inside an abandoned house. The roof of the house had collapsed to reveal the animal, which was tied to one of its pillars. If the villager had not been on top of the tall tree, he would never have spotted the buffalo. It turned out that a thief in the town was stealing livestock and hiding them in an abandoned house. He would wait for nightfall and then lead the animals to another village to be sold.

On the same day that the villager found his buffalo, a boy of thirteen or fourteen years old asked Wang Ch'ung-yang, "My brother has been away from the village for a long time, and we have not received any messages. Can you tell me when he will return?" Wang Ch'ung-yang replied, "Go home and ask your mother." The child ran off, not believing what Wang Ch'ung-yang told him. As he entered the house, he saw his mother holding a letter. Seeing her son, the mother called to him and said, "My son, come and read this letter to me. The messenger said that it came from your brother." The child read aloud, "To my mother: Greetings. Since my father's death you have brought me up and taught me to be an honorable man. Now I have a chance to carry on the business that father has left me. I have traveled far and have made many successful business transactions. Because there has been a delay in a shipment of some goods, I shall not be able to return by the date that I have promised. Please do not worry about me. When the autumn wind blows, around the middle of the ninth month I shall be home." The child had scarcely finished reading when he clapped his hands and said, "This is incredible! This is incredible!" His mother was about to ask him what was so incredible when she heard the voices of five or six men at the door.

12

When the boy opened the door, one of the men asked if he knew the way to the Ma mansion. The boy said, "If you are going to the Ma mansion, then you must be looking for the immortal." The men said, "Yes, we have come a long way to see him." The boy said, "I know the way. It is not far from here. I'll take you there."

They arrived at the Ma mansion and, entering through the front door, saw Ma Tan-yang, who greeted them. When the men informed him that they had come to seek the teacher of the Tao, he led them through the back garden to the meditation hall. In this group was a man called T'an Ch'u-tuan. His Taoist name was T'an Ch'ang-chen, meaning "eternal enlightenment." He had met Wang Ch'ung-yang a few years earlier when Wang Ch'ung-yang had journeyed from Shensi Province to Shantung. T'an Ch'ang-chen had had a weak constitution and was severely ill at the time. Wang Ch'ung-yang taught him certain Taoist practices for strengtening his immunity to disease. T'an Ch'ang-chen not only made a remarkable recovery but found that in the years since he had practiced the techniques, his health had improved dramatically. He had wanted to seek out Wang Ch'ung-yang to study with him, but only now, when Wang Ch'ung-yang's fame began to spread in Shantung Province, had he been able to obtain information as to the master's whereabouts. When he heard that Wang Ch'ung-yang was at the Ma mansion he immediately sought out Hao Ta-t'ung, a friend of his who had wanted to study the teachings of the Tao but had not been able to find a master. Hao Ta-t'ung would later be known by his Taoist name Hao T'ai-ku, meaning "the ancient way." Together the two friends journeyed from their village to the county of Ning-hai, and along the way they were joined by others who had heard of Wang Ch'ung-yang's fame and wanted to meet him.

When T'an Ch'ang-chen saw Wang Ch'ung-yang he bowed low and thanked the master for having cured him a few years earlier. He then said, "Sir, now that my health allows it, I would like to spend my life studying the teachings of the Tao with you." Wang Ch'ung-yang replied, "The teachings of the Tao are open to all. You are free to take what you can. Those who come are not turned away. Those who leave will not be forced to stay." Turning to Ma Tan-yang, he said, "Show them to their meditation huts."

A few days later two men arrived at the Ma mansion. One was named Liu Ch'u-yüan. His Taoist name was Liu Ch'ang-sheng, meaning "eternal life." He was accompanied by a friend whose name was Wang Ch'u-i. Wang Ch'u-i would later be known by the Taoist name Wang Yü-yang, meaning "jade *yang*." When they expressed their wish to study with Wang Ch'ung-yang, Ma Tan-yang escorted them through the back garden to their meditation huts.

As time went on, more and more people gathered at the Ma mansion. Wang Ch'ung-yang then told Ma Tan-yang to set up regulations and guidelines for training. Duties were allocated, and a training schedule was set up. Thus, in a few years' time, the Ma mansion became a center of learning for seekers of the Tao, just as Wang Ch'ung-yang had planned.

One day Wang Ch'ung-yang gathered all the students together in the meditation hall and expounded to them the principles of Taoist meditation. He said, "*Ch'i,* or original breath, is the foundation of life. The heart is the source of the foundation, and original nature is the prerequisite for building that foundation. The distance between Heaven and earth is said to be eighty-four thousand miles. The distance between the heart and the kidneys is eight and four-tenths inches. The kidneys are the "internal kidneys," that is, a region three inches below the navel. Here all the channels of the body meet. Let the breath hover there, and all channels will open when you exhale and will close when you inhale. The mysteries of Heaven and earth are all embodied in inhalation and exhalation. If breathing involves the region of the body between the heart and the kidneys, then your blood will be healthy and circulation will be smooth. If the emotions are dissolved, then all your illnesses will be cured without herbs.

"You should try to sit and meditate at the hours *tzu, wu, mao,* and *yu* (11:00 P.M.–1:00 A.M, 11:00 A.M.–1:00 P.M., 5:00 A.M.– 7:00 A.M., 5:00 P.M.–7:00 P.M.). Sit cross-legged on a cushion or

指坐工，申
明妙理
學真道喜
遇明師
于植 [印]

Wang Ch'ung-yang expounds the methods of Taoist meditation.
Five seekers of the Tao meet their teacher.

68

blanket. Gently stop up your ears with cotton and stop all internal conversation. Let your breathing be natural. Each exhalation and inhalation should be unhurried. Let your eyes drop and focus on the region three inches below the navel. Sit for a period of one incense stick. When you feel that the breathing is smooth, you should sit for another period of one incense stick. When you feel that your breathing is quiet and slow, then slowly uncross your legs and remove the cotton from your ears. Sit relaxed for a while, and then walk slowly around the room. After a while you may eat half a bowl of soup or rice. Do not engage in rigorous activities that engage the body or mind. Otherwise this will undo whatever progress you have made in your meditation."

In another region of Shantung there lived a man by the name of Ch'iu Ch'u-chi. His parents had died when he was young, and he had been brought up by his two elder brothers. Ch'iu Ch'u-chi showed himself to be a promising student in the village school. He excelled in poetry, calligraphy, and the classics. However, he was not interested in pursuing a career in government service. While other young men aspired to wealth and fame, he preferred to seek out quiet places, where he would sit and contemplate. When his brothers tried to rouse his interest in the civil service, Ch'iu Ch'u-chi replied, "Fame and wealth are impermanent. True pursuit of knowledge should not be directed toward material gains." Seeing that their younger brother could not be persuaded to enter government office, they next tried to interest him in the responsibilities of raising a family. To this he replied, "A man should do great deeds before committing himself to a family." He then added, "We are born in this world with a purpose. And the purpose is not to fight for wealth and fame. Fame and fortune are like dust. People think that material goods are everything but I see them as ripples on the water or clouds in the sky. We may possess them for a while, but we must discard them when we die."

His brothers saw that Ch'iu Ch'u-chi was no ordinary person, although he subscribed to beliefs that were considered strange by his contemporaries. Thus they said among themselves, "Let us not force him any longer. Maybe he is destined to pursue a path different from us mortals."

One day Ch'iu Ch'u-chi overheard a conversation in the marketplace alluding to Wang Ch'ung-yang's remarkable abilities and his reputation as a teacher of the Tao. He saw that this would be his chance to learn from a Taoist master. He decided to journey to the Ma mansion in Ning-hai County and beg this teacher to receive him as a disciple. However, he was afraid that his brothers might not be receptive to his plans, so without informing them of his plans he quietly packed a few belongings for the road and slipped out of the village at night.

As Ch'iu Ch'u-chi arrived at the Ma mansion, he met Ma Tan-yang, who greeted him and introduced him to Liu Ch'ang-sheng and Hao T'ai-ku. They welcomed him warmly and said, "It is rare that a young man of such good looks and intelligence is drawn toward the teachings of the Tao. We are delighted to have you here." Ma Tan-Yang then took Ch'iu Ch'u-chi to meet Wang Ch'ung-yang. When he explained to his teacher that the young man wished to cultivate the Tao, Wang Ch'ung-yang eyed Ch'iu Ch'u-chi intently and then shook his head. "This one's mind is too lively, and his intelligence is too sharp. It would be better for him to go home now. Otherwise, his staying will lead to many problems." Ch'iu Ch'u-chi bowed and knelt down. "Sir, there is nothing else that I want to do but study the teachings of the Tao. Please reconsider and receive me as a student." Wang Ch'ung-yang waved his hand to tell Ch'iu Ch'u-chi to leave. Ch'iu Ch'u-chi stepped out of the meditation hall but was reluctant to leave the mansion. Seeing the young man's sincerity, Ma Tan-yang pleaded for him. But Wang Ch'ung-yang explained to his senior disciple, "It is not that my heart is hard and I do not want to teach him. This young man has much suffering waiting for him if he decides to pursue the path of immortality. I fear that he may not be able to bear the brunt of the sufferings and thus may leave the path with misgivings and regret. In the end this will hurt his karma more than if he had never heard of the Tao. Thus I would rather have him leave now and not have the chance to incur serious karmic retribution."

Ma Tan-yang found Ch'iu Ch'u-chi sitting in the living room, dejected and sad. He did not have the heart to turn him away, so he invited Ch'iu Ch'u-chi to stay on in the Ma mansion as an errand boy. Ch'iu Ch'u-chi accepted this gratefully and performed his chores with diligence. Occasionally Ma Tan-yang taught him meditation, giving him some of the basics of Taoist training. One day, Ch'iu Ch'u-chi said to Ma Tan-yang, "Sir, you have been very kind to me, and I am very grateful. It looks as though I will not be able to study with Master Wang in this lifetime. May I ask you to be my teacher instead?" Ma Tan-yang said, "I cannot be your teacher. When you seek the Tao, you must find an enlightened master to guide you. I am not an enlightened teacher. I know only some of the introductory techniques. As for guiding you in the path of the Tao, I am incapable of such a task. My learning is still shallow and my training inadequate. However, do not despair. When I see the chance I shall speak with the master again and ask him to receive you as a disciple." Ch'iu Ch'u-chi thanked Ma Tan-yang many times and became a member of the community of Taoists in the Ma mansion.

Ch'iu Ch'u-chi proved to be a hardworking and conscientious helper in the household. He accepted duties cheerfully and good-naturedly. He was polite and friendly. Everyone in the community liked this new servant and agreed that he added much joy and vitality to the household.

One day Wang Ch'ung-yang called his disciples to the meditation hall. The students stood in two columns facing the master and listened attentively. Meanwhile, unnoticed, Ch'iu Ch'u-chi stood outside the meditation hall under a window and listened to the master's teachings.

Wang Ch'ung-yang said, "I came all the way here to Shantung Province to impart the teachings of the Tao to the world. My goal is to let everyone hear the teachings so that they may return to the path of the Tao. I have seen the intelligent, the stupid, the ignorant, and the well-educated. I have been called a genius by some and labeled insane by others. You may say that I am stupid, ignorant, and dull-witted. Why am I stupid? Because in my stupidity I do not know how to desire and covet. Why am I ignorant? Because in my ignorance I am not rashful and impatient. Why am I dull-witted? Because of my dull wits I am incapable of fabricating schemes to outwit and outdo others.

Being stupid and ignorant has made me impervious to the attraction of material things. You may think this is strange, but I am merely teaching you to be stupid, ignorant, and dull-witted. If you do not know your heart, you do not know the Tao. Therefore, to cultivate the Tao, you must first start with cultivating the heart. You must replace a heart of stray thoughts and desire with a heart of the Tao. Still your thoughts and calm your mind. Tame the wildness in you until nothing can cause your mind to move. Taming the heart is not easy. You must be on guard constantly. When you notice your mind moving, you should calm it. Only through this can you build a strong foundation. The mystery of the Tao is in the emptiness of mind. Dissolve your thoughts, and the original breath of life will emerge. The heart belongs to the element fire, and fire has both *yin* and *yang* components. The symbol of fire is two solid lines (*yang*) flanking one broken line (*yin*): ☲ *Yang* and *yin* need each other to copulate and produce the Golden Pill. Thoughts residing in the mind are like monsters. They are obstacles that prevent you from attaining the Tao. If you are unable to still your mind, then you can accomplish nothing and the Tao will be farther away than ever."

While Wang Ch'ung-yang was expounding the importance of calming the mind to his students, Ch'iu Ch'u-chi was so engrossed in listening that he forgot he was not supposed to be sneaking around outside the meditation hall. At the top of his voice he cried, "That's right, that's right! That's what I need to do!" Wang Ch'ung-yang stopped the lesson and returned to his room. When the students saw Ch'iu Ch'u-chi standing sheepishly outside the hall they reprimanded him, saying that Master Wang had stopped his lesson because he was interrupted by an uninvited listener. Ch'iu Ch'u-chi accepted the angry words with silence. All this time he was thinking to himself. "The master talked about the cultivation and taming of the heart. But he was really referring to the cultivation of the Tao because the Tao is in the heart. so, to attain the Tao, I must first tame my heart." From that day on, Ch'iu Ch'u-chi watched his actions carefully and tried to practice Wang Ch'ung-yang's instructions in his daily life.

13

The next day Ch'iu Ch'u-chi again followed the other students to the meditation hall. Again he listened under a window.

That day Wang Ch'ung-yang expounded on the importance of dissolving self-interest. He said, "Those who cultivate the Tao must attend to every detail of their daily lives. If there is a trace of self-interest, the heart is still impure and an obstacle still stands in the way between you and the Tao. As self-interest arises, Earlier Heaven is lost. When Earlier Heaven is lost, so will the original breath of life disappear. Self-interest is like evil fire. When evil fire burns in you, the original breath dissolves. How can the true fires which heat the herbs arise when evil fire is in their place? How can the true spirit emerge if the original breath of life is blocked by self-importance? Now that you know this, would you try to dissolve self-interest? Would you try to tame your wild thoughts? Your mind must not be moved by attachments. Only in the absence of attachments can stillness be cultivated. In stillness, the *yang* spirit will grow and the impurities in your body will decrease. It is through stillness that the Taoist immortals and bodhisattvas attain their enlightenment."

Again Ch'iu Ch'u-chi could not control his reaction, and his loud exclamations brought the teacher's lesson to a halt. This time Wang Ch'ung-yang asked that the culprit be brought into the hall. When Wang Ch'ung-yang saw who it was, he turned to Ma Tan-yang and said angrily, "I told you to see to it that he returned to his home. Why is he still here?" Liu Ch'ang-sheng, Hao T'ai-ku, Wang Yü-yang, and T'an Ch'ang-chen all pleaded for Ch'iu Ch'u-chi, saying, "Ch'iu Ch'u-chi sincerely came to seek the Tao. Please let him stay." Wang Ch'ung-yang said, "I told him to leave because I am afraid he may not be able to bear the sufferings that he will encounter in his pursuit of enlightenment. I don't want him to leave the path with regret when the things become difficult. It will bring on him karmic retribution." Liu Ch'ang-sheng pleaded again. Finally, Wang Ch'ung-yang said, "All right, I shall accept him as a disciple." Turning to Ma

Tan-yang and the others he said, "I shall entrust him to you. Look after him and see that he does not get into trouble." Wang Ch'ung-yang then gave Ch'iu Ch'u-chi the Taoist name of Ch'iu Ch'ang-ch'un, meaning "eternal spring." After a brief initiation ceremony, Ch'iu Ch'ang-ch'un officially joined the brotherhood of Wang Ch'ung-yang's disciples.

A few months later, Wang Ch'ung-yang told Ma Tan-yang, "Gather all the students outside the meditation hall and set up an altar. I wish to speak to all of them there." The students gathered and stood respectfully in their ranks. Wang Ch'ung-yang took a seat in front of the altar and spoke.

"Today I shall expound the meaning of stillness. If you understand the meaning of stillness not only will you understand the Tao, but you will be able to manage a family and rule a kingdom. There is deep meaning hidden in the word "stillness." Many talk about stillness, but few really understand it. To get to the root of stillness one must view the world as empty. One enters stillness through severing ties to whatever disrupts stillness. When you are in a state of stillness you need to be alert and must dissolve stray thoughts before they contaminate the stillness. In this way, distractions will disappear before they arise. What do we mean by maintaining stillness? True stillness is when a mountain crashes in front of you and you are not afraid. It is when a pretty woman or handsome man stands in front of you and your desires are not roused. In stillness a parent can patiently teach a wayward child. In stillness an elder sibling can instruct the younger. In stillness husband and wife can live in harmony. In stillness friends can open their minds to each other. In stillness the ruler can attend to the welfare of the ruled. Thus, stillness is the center of activity, yet in activity there is stillness. The Buddhists say, 'Clear the mind and see original nature.' Only in stillness can the mind be cleared and original nature be seen. The Confucianists say, 'Know the depths of your nature through reason.' Only in stillness can reason reach the depths of your nature. The Taoists say, 'Cultivate your true nature and tame your heart.' Only in stillness can the heart be tamed and true nature be cultivated. Therefore, the cultivation of stillness is the foundation of the Three Religions [Confucianism, Buddhism,

散壇場學
入通家去
換道裝師
徒往南來

*Wang Ch'ung-yang disbands the retreat and travels with
his disciples.*

Taoism]. Just as the movement in spring is preceded by the stillness of winter, it is in stillness that spontaneous action is born."

When Wang Ch'ung-yang finished speaking and looked at the crowd of students, he knew that only six of them would eventually attain the Tao. They were Ch'iu Ch'ang-ch'un, Liu Ch'ang-sheng, Wang Yü-yang, T'an Ch'ang-chen, Ma Tan-yang, and Hao T'ai-ku. The rest of the students would sooner or later abandon the path. For some, their enthusiasm would wear out. Others would not have the discipline. And for most, the attractions of the material world would prove stronger than their motivation to cultivate the Tao. He gave his followers the lesson of stillness so that even those who discontinued their Taoist training could benefit from the teachings and lead virtuous lives.

The master had scarcely finished speaking when Ch'iu Ch'ang-ch'un could not contain himself and started talking loudly to some of the students about what he thought were the implications of Wang Ch'ung-yang's lesson. Wang Ch'ung-yang looked toward Ch'iu Ch'ang-ch'un and said in a stern voice, "You have listened to the teachings of the Tao, and yet you have not altered your bad habits. You have been instructed in the principles of the cultivation of the heart, and yet you have not understood. You think you are intelligent, but you show total ignorance of everything I have taught you. You jump to conclusions without thinking. You play with ideas but never put them into practice. You have broken regulations and rules of training time after time. I do not want to be bothered with you any longer. Tomorrow I shall go south to visit some friends. Liu Ch'ang-sheng, Wang Yü-yang, T'an Ch'ang-chen, and Hao T'ai-ku will accompany me. Ma Tan-yang will stay at the mansion and take care of things while I am away. The rest of the students may stay or leave. I shall be back in a year's time."

That evening, most of the students packed their belongings and planned to return home. Many were homesick and wanted to see their parents, spouses, and children. By dawn almost everyone was gone. Ma Tan-yang prepared five sets of Taoist robes, straw hats, and sandals for his teacher and his four fellow disciples. Dressed as wandering medicant Taoist monks, the party quietly left the Ma mansion. Ma Tan-yang followed his master for a short distance and said farewell at the edge of town. Turning toward home, he saw Ch'iu Ch'ang-ch'un. "What are you doing here?" Ma Tan-yang inquired. Ch'iu Ch'ang-ch'un said, "I am following the master." Ma Tan-yang said, "Did you not hear that the teacher decided to leave because he was annoyed by your behavior? If you insist on going with him, it will make him unhappy." Ch'iu Ch'ang-ch'un said, "I know that the master is not really angry with me. He scolded me because he wanted me to learn. If I did not follow him, I would be ungrateful." Ma Tan-yang said, "You cannot go like this. You are not dressed in Taoist robes. It would cause the master and the others a lot of trouble if you dressed differently. Let us go back to the mansion and I shall get you the appropriate garb." Ch'iu Ch'ang-ch'un thanked Ma Tan-yang gratefully. Soon Ch'iu Ch'ang-ch'un was cloaked in Taoist robes; hurrying down the road, he soon caught sight of Wang Ch'ung-yang and the others.

14

When Ch'iu Ch'ang=ch'un caught up with Wang Ch'ung-yang's party it was early evening. They had walked all day and had not stopped to eat. Now that they were near a village Ch'iu Ch'ang-ch'un thought that he might try to beg some rice and vegetables for his master. He did not know how to beg as a monk, but he decided to try. Timidly he knocked on the door of a house. Dogs barked, and a farmer opened the door. When he saw Ch'iu Ch'ang-ch'un's monkish garb, he disappeared inside and soon returned with a bowl of rice. Ch'iu Ch'ang-ch'un begged from several houses and had more than enough food for his master. He hurried ahead and found Wang Ch'ung-yang and the others sitting under a tree. As he approached, he saw his master speaking to Liu Ch'ang-sheng and Hao T'ai-ku: "It is evening and we have walked all day. Did you bring enough money to buy food?" Liu Ch'ang-sheng said, "Sir, we were in a hurry when we left and forgot to prepare finances for the journey." Wang Ch'ung-yang said, "If we have no money you must all go to the village and beg for food. I shall wait for you here."

When Wang Ch'ung-yang was alone, Ch'iu Ch'ang-ch'un stepped forward and offered his teacher the rice and vegetables that he had begged from three kind-hearted villagers. Wang Ch'ung-yang looked at Ch'iu Ch'ang-ch'un angrily and said, "I do not want to be bothered by you. Take your food away." Ch'iu Ch'ang-ch'un tried to present the food to his master again, but Wang Ch'ung-yang turned and walked away.

Presently the four disciples returned. They each had managed to obtain some rice and corn. Liu Ch'ang-sheng presented his share to Wang Ch'ung-yang. The master sat down, nibbled a few morsels, and gave it back to his disciple. The disciples ate a meager meal and continued the journey. Late at night they arrived at an abandoned shrine. Liu Ch'ang-sheng and the other disciples cleaned out a corner and placed the master's meditation mat there. Wang Ch'ung-yang meditated through the night while the others slept. The next day they rose early and continued their way.

All this time Ch'iu Ch'ang-ch'un was following behind them. They reached another village, and as Ch'iu Ch'ang-ch'un was walking past a rice field a farmer called out to him, "Young master, stop by my home and we will be honored to have dinner with a Taoist monk." Ch'iu Ch'ang-ch'un thanked him for his kindness and said, "My master and my elder brothers are ahead of me on the road, and they have not stopped for dinner yet. How can I eat with you and ignore my teacher?" The farmer replied, "That is not a problem. You can still eat with my family, and we shall cook something extra for you to take to your teacher and brothers." Ch'iu Ch'ang-ch'un ate a full meal at the farmer's house and then packed five shares of rice and vegetables for Wang Ch'ung-yang and the others.

Ch'iu Ch'ang-ch'un soon caught up with the others. Wang Ch'ung-yang had just told the disciples to beg from the nearby houses. Respectfully Ch'iu Ch'ang-ch'un offered hs master the rice and vegetables prepared by the generous farmer. Wang Ch'ung-yang looked at the package of food and said, "This comes from one family. I do not want to eat it. Do you not know the rules of begging? The food must come from many homes, not just one." He turned away and walked away from Ch'iu Ch'ang-ch'un. Ch'iu Ch'ang-ch'un did not know what to do. His master would not eat what he had begged. To return the food to the kind family would make them feel rejected. In any case, it would be a long way there and back and he would not be able to find his master and the others again if he left them. He stood there trembling and sweating for a long time. He was in despair when he saw his elder brothers returning. They had had little luck getting food and they welcomed Ch'iu Ch'ang-ch'un's share of rice and vegetables. The bowls were soon emptied, and night was falling as they took to the road again.

Ch'iu Ch'ang-ch'un thought ot himself, "My teacher comes from Shensi Province. Of course he has no appetite for rice. Tomorrow I shall try to beg some bread and noodles for him." The next day Ch'iu Ch'ang-ch'un managed to get some bread as they passed through a small town. He presented the loaf to Wang Ch'ung-yang, but the master said, "I told you that I would not

Wang Ch'ung-yang tests Ch'iu Ch'ang-ch'un.

eat what you begged, so get out of my sight." He turned and walked away briskly.

Why did Wang Ch'ung-yang behave harshly to Ch'iu Ch'ang-ch'un and ignore hs goodwill? Wang Ch'ung-yang had his reasons. Ch'iu Ch'ang-ch'un was the youngest of all his disciples. Unlike Ma Tan-yang, Liu Ch'ang-sheng, and the others, Ch'iu Ch'ang-ch'un had not experienced enough of life to have his heart tempered through hardship. Thus Ch'iu Ch'ang-ch'un needed to be exposed to hardships and have his temper tested over and over again until Wang Ch'ung-yang could be satisfied that his student was made of the caliber of one who would attain the Tao. But Ch'iu Ch'ang-ch'un was an extraordinary person. Although young, he had a strong foundation and did not succumb to the trials that his master put him through. Not only was he not provoked to anger and resentment, but he bore the hardships with continued respect and consideration for his teacher and his elder brothers.

Two months passed, and winter set in. The weather turned cold. Snow began to fall. One evening the disciples collected some firewood and built a small fire in the main hall of an abandoned temple. Eagerly, each of them warmed his bowl of food by the fire. When Wang Ch'ung-yang saw this, he threw the entire bundle of dry branches into the fire. The flames leapt up, and smoke filled the room. Sputtering and coughing, the disciples ran out of the room into the temple courtyard. Swiftly Wang Ch'ung-yang closed the door and bolted it. The disciples were left out in the cold. They tried to push open the door but it would not budge. Afraid to disturb their teacher's meditation, they huddled together and shivered. Liu Ch'ang-sheng suddenly remembered that their teacher had taught them how to circulate their internal energy to keep warm and suggested to the others that they should try this to see if the technique could keep them warm.

After circulating their internal energy for a while, the disciples began to feel heat inside their bodies. They sat in the temple courtyard until dawn.

When the sun rose, Wang Ch'ung-yang opened the door of the temple. The students filed into the main hall and Wang Ch'ung-yang said sternly, "You cannot stand the heat and smoke, and you are afraid of the cold. You want to keep warm the easy way by heating your food and sitting near a fire, not knowing that the true fire is within yourself. You are lazy and soft and undisciplined. If you cannot bear hardship, if you are unwilling to practice what I taught you, then how can you expect to attain the Tao?" Turning to Wang Yü-yang, the master said, "Bring me the discipline rod. For your behavior last night, you all deserve twenty strokes." The disciples stood silently and waited for their punishment. Ch'iu Ch'ang-ch'un knelt down in front of his teacher and pleaded, "Sir, building a fire and heating food were my ideas. It was all my fault. I am willing to take all the punishment." Wang Ch'ung-yang looked at him intently and said, "If you are willing to take their punishment, then you will receive a total of one hundred strokes, twenty each for the four of them and twenty for yourself." Hearing the master's remark, Liu Ch'ang-sheng, Hao T'ai-ku, Wang Yü-yang, and T'an Ch'ang-chen all begged Wang Ch'ung-yang to spare Ch'iu Ch'ang-ch'un. Together they all knelt down before the master and begged that they be beaten instead. Wang Ch'ung-yang looked at them, sighed and said, "You all have brotherly love for each other. I shall spare everyone this time. But remember, do not repeat your mistakes." Turning to Liu Ch'ang-sheng he said, "I have lost enthusiasm for the journey. We shall not continue south. Let us return to Shantung now." The disciples gathered their belongings, said farewell to the caretaker of the broken-down temple, and traced their route back to Ning-hai County. Ch'iu Ch'ang-ch'un went ahead of the others to the Ma mansion to inform Ma Tan-yang of the teacher's return.

15

When it was known that Wang Ch'ung-yang had returned to the Ma mansion, the people who had left began to return. Within a few days, the Ma mansion was bustling with activity. Although everyone's former enthusiasm appeared to be renewed, Wang Ch'ung-yang saw that almost all who were there were either insincere or not disciplined enough in their pursuit of the Tao. He thought to himself, "These people are here because their interest was roused at the moment, or because they are afraid of dying, or because they are following the crowd. None of them have the discipline and sincerity to cultivate the Tao. If they continue to stay, they will distract those who are sincere. I must find a way to make them leave." After a few moments, he said, "That's it. I have a plan." Immediately he started to cough violently, emitting loud, gurgling sounds. When the disciples came running to his room, Wang Ch'ung-yang said, "I was not careful on the road, and I must have gotten a strange infection." Opening his tunic, he revealed rashes and boils all over his body. Ma Tan-yang, Liu Ch'ang-sheng, and Ch'iu Ch'ang-ch'un immediately went to fetch a doctor. Wang Ch'ung-yang took the prescribed medicine, but the rashes and boils got worse: Pus flowed from the rashes, and few could stand the stench.

Many of the students began to whisper among themselves, "We came to learn from an immortal. Wang Ch'ung-yang is so ill that he cannot even save himself. How can he help us? Maybe we should go home or find another teacher. We are wasting our time here." So one by one, the students began to leave. Within two days, all the students had left except for Ma Tan-yang, Ch'iu Ch'ang-ch'un, Liu Ch'ang-sheng, Hao T'ai-ku, T'an Ch'ang-chen, and Wang Yü-yang. Wang Ch'ung-yang summoned them to his room and said, "Tomorrow at 11:00 A.M. I shall die. Since my arrival at Ma Tan-yang's home, I have spent his wealth helping the poor and building a retreat. Almost all of the money is gone now. An elaborate funeral costs money, and you should not sell property to cover the expenses. Therefore, after I die, do not arrange for funeral ceremonies or have monks chant for me. Do not even mourn for me. Get a coffin and put my body in it. Ch'iu Ch'ang-ch'un, T'an Ch'ang-chen, Hao T'ai-ku, and Wang Yü-yang will carry the coffin. Liu Ch'ang-sheng will lead the group to Mount Chung-nan in Shensi Province. The place where the carrying-ropes break will be where I should be buried. If you do not follow my request I shall not rest in peace."

The next morning Wang Ch'ung-yang assembled his six disciples in the meditation hall and spoke to them: "The dual cultivation of life and of original nature (mind) is the essence of my teachings. If you cultivate life only, your virtues will be incomplete. If you cultivate the mind only, your body will be impure. Therefore, you should balance your external and internal training. Externally, you must be careful with all your actions. Be careful of what you say, what you think, what you do, and how you feel. Watch your intentions. Your mind should be empty of desire. Internally, you should dissolve all ideas of form. The techniques of cultivating the internals cannot be grasped through form. If you retain even one speck of form, your fires will not be truly *yang,* and your body will not be pure. The obstacles to training are laziness, impatience, and desire for results. Consequently people stagnate in their development, or try to practice techniques that are way beyond their ability, or are too attached to progress. Not only can they not attain the Tao, but they will risk danger and harm to the body."

Wang Ch'ung-yang then presented a book to Ma Tan-yang and said, "This book contains my teachings. It shows you ways of cultivating the Tao. The six of you should consult it often. It will advise you as to what to do when you encounter problems. The theory behind the techniques is easy to understand. The difficulty of these methods lies in the practice. You do not have to worry about your friend Sun Pu-erh. She is well on her way to becoming an immortal. I no longer need to worry about her. But each of you here will meet with obstacles in your training. Liu Ch'ang-sheng, you have not emptied your mind of forms and sexual attraction. Hao T'ai-ku, you must wander east and west but you will not attain the Tao until you have climbed the cliff-

示羽化
仙師通
隱送靈
柩門人
服勞
于柩

Wang Ch'ung-yang sheds his bodily shell and leaves the mortal realm. The disciples carry their teacher's bier to Shensi for burial.

edged mountains. T'an Ch'ang-chen, your meeting with one named Ku will show that you still cling to preconceptions. Wang Yü-yang, your powers will not mature until you meet with one named Yao. Ch'iu Ch'ang-ch'un, your hardships will not end until you reach the river that flows over many boulders." After speaking these words, Wang Ch'ung-yang stopped breathing.

The disciples followed Wang Ch'ung-yang's instructions and put his body in a coffin. They tied carrying ropes around it, and the next morning, led by Liu Ch'ang-sheng, Chiu Ch'ang-ch'un, Hao T'ai-ku, T'an Ch'ang-chen, and Wang Yü-yang carried his coffin and began their long walk to Shensi.

Along the way, the disciples met many people who wished to pay their last respects to the teacher. Some were Wang Ch'ung-yang's former students, the very same ones who had abandoned him when they discovered he was ailing. Others had heard of Wang Ch'ung-yang's fame and were simply curious. However, in his lifetime Wang Ch'ung-yang had always detested people with insincere interest. When these people approached the bier, a stench oozed from the coffin. The crowd soon dispersed. From then on, whenever crowds of curious people gathered around the bier, unbearable odors would exude from the coffin, driving them away.

As the disciples journeyed westward, they discovered that there were always well-wishers who provided meals for them every day. Even when they were far from settlements, someone would approach them on the road and offer them rice and vegetables. Moreover, they seemed to be able to find an abandoned house or shrine for shelter every night.

One night, after two months on the road, Ch'iu Ch'ang-ch'un began to think that something strange was going on. He thought to himself, "In Shantung the master had many admirers, so it was not strange that there were well-wishers providing us with food every day. But now we are in regions in which the master was not well known. How is it that we still meet with so many well-wishers on the road? Something weird must be going on."

Around noon the next day the disciples saw someone approaching them with two baskets of food. While Liu Ch'ang-sheng thanked the man and the other disciples began to eat, Ch'iu

Ch'ang-ch'un softly asked their benefactor, "How do you know we are here? Why are you bringing us food?" The man replied, "This morning a Taoist monk dressed in yellow robes came to my home and told me to take enough food to give five Taoist monks who were bearing a coffin. He also told me that around noontime they should be on the road ten miles from my home and that if I did this good deed the gods would reward me."

Early next morning, as the disciples were about to set out, Ch'iu Ch'ang-ch'un approached Liu Ch'ang-sheng and said, "Brother, I have a bad stomachache, and I need to hurry to the next town to get some medicine. Could you carry the teacher's bier for me while I run ahead?" The good-natured Liu Ch'ang-sheng suspected nothing and consented to Ch'iu Ch'ang-ch'un's request. While the others walked slowly along, Ch'iu Ch'ang-ch'un ran into the nearest town. As he approached the market-place he saw a Taoist monk dressed in yellow robes. After following the monk for a while, he recognized that the monk's voice and gait resembled his master's. Ch'iu Ch'ang-ch'un could not bear it any more. He walked up behind the monk and said, "Master, your student is here to serve you." Wang Ch'ung-yang turned around and said, "You fool! You do not understand the importance of keeping the secrets of Heaven. Now you have ruined everything. And you have planted more obstacles for yourself in your pursuit of the Tao." Wang Ch'ung-yang then disappeared.

Ch'iu Ch'ang-ch'un repented of his folly, but it was too late. From then on, no one met the disciples and provided meals for them, and abandoned dwellings were hard to find. The disciples were forced to spend the small amount of money that Ma Tan-yang had given them. Half a month passed. When they arrived at the city of Changan, they had spent almost all their money. Fortunately, they were nearing their destination, for Mount Chung-nan was not far away.

One day, as they were approaching an area of lovely rolling hills and thickly wooded slopes, the carrying ropes on the bier broke. While the disciples were carefully setting the coffin on the ground, an old man walked up to them and said, "Are you the ones who have walked all the way from Shantung Province with this coffin?" Ch'iu Ch'ang-ch'un said, "Yes, indeed we are." The old man then said, "Last night I had a dream in which my friend Wang T'ieh-hsin told me that he had died and that his disciples would arrive with his body the next day. He then asked me to give him a plot of my land to be his burial place. Wang T'ieh-hsien and I were good friends. We studied together in the village school and then went on to take the imperial examinations. I told him that I would be honored to carry out his last wish. Then I asked him when his disciples would arrive and he told me that they would be here at noon. The dream was so vivid that when I woke up I decided to come here and wait for you."

Ch'iu Ch'ang-ch'un then related to the old man Wang Ch'ung-yang's wish to be buried at Mount Chung-nan at the place where the carrying ropes broke. The old man said, "Your master's coffin is now resting on land that is my property. Let us honor your master's last wish and bury him here." He beckoned to his servants and told them to dig a burial hole. The disciples administered last rites for Wang Ch'ung-yang, and the coffin was lowered slowly into the ground. A burial mound was erected, and as the disciples were preparing to leave, the old man said, "Come to my home for dinner." The disciples accepted the old man's invitation; after the dinner, Ch'iu Ch'ang-ch'un and Liu Ch'ang-sheng asked for directions to Wang Ch'ung-yang's home village, for they deemed it proper to notify Wang Ch'ung-yang's relatives of his passing.

16

Ch'iu Ch'ang-ch'un and the other disciples arrived at Ta-wei Village. Instead of a prosperous town, they saw broken-down buildings and abandoned farms. The once-fertile fields were now overgrown with weeds. They walked to the middle of town, looking for residents who might have known their master's family. The once-busy market place was deserted. Shops were boarded up, and even the trees appeared wilted. At one corner of the marketplace the disciples noticed three old men sitting on the steps of a small shrine. Ch'iu Ch'ang-ch'un approached them, bowed politely, and asked, "Sirs, would you know which house belonged to Wang T'ieh-hsin?" One of the old men replied, "Who are you, and why do you ask of Wang T'ieh-hsin?" Ch'iu Ch'ang-ch'un said, "We are disciples of one Wang Ch'ung-yang, who was known in his home village as Wang T'ieh-hsin. Our master ascended to the immortal realm in Shantung. We bore his body to Shensi to be buried in Mount Chung-nan according to his wishes. We came to notify his family and relatives of his passing." The old man sighed and said, "Your master was my cousin. Much has happened since he left here a long time ago. Not long after he disappeared mysteriously, his wife died of grief. His son went to live in his father-in-law's village and only returns to visit once in a while. There is nobody living in the Wang mansion now." The second old man added, "Since Master Wang left the village everything went to pieces. You see, Master Wang was a responsible man. He helped the poor, supervised the public works and acted as a judge when there were petty quarrels. When he left there was nobody here to take care of things. People looked only after their own concerns. For example, people swept only the snow in front of their houses. As a result, the dams were not repaired, the irrigation ditches were unattended, the fields became fallow, and people moved away. Then some people began to blame Master Wang, saying that he had gone and become an immortal and had taken the spirit of the village when he left."

Ch'iu Ch'ang-ch'un then asked the old men, "How did you know our master became an immortal?" The old man who was Wang Ch'ung-yang's cousin said, "See this shrine? It is dedicated to Master Wang. He is revered throughout this area because of the deeds he has done. Go into the shrine and read the memorial plaques." The disciples went into the shrine and saw a statue in the likeness of their master. In front of the statue were offerings of food and incense. Despite the desolate feel of the village, the shrine appeared to have been tended constantly. Two inscribed plaques flanked the statue. Ch'iu Ch'ang-ch'un read aloud: "The immortal showed his Taoist powers in the city of Han-yang. He saved a town from fire with a cup of wine. He has not forgotten his ancestral village, for his talismans saved our village from the plague." Liu Ch'ang-sheng asked the old men what the writings were referring to. One of the old men explained, "Many years ago a plague ran through the area. We were afraid that it would wipe out the entire village. One day a Taoist monk dressed in yellow robes was seen placing talismans on the doors of the houses. Those who were ill with the plague were cured, and those who were well were not touched by the dreaded sickness when the plague passed through this region. We have also heard that in the city of Han-yang a fire threatened to burn down large sections of the town. Suddenly, a Taoist monk in yellow robes appeared. He took a sip of wine from a bottle and spit it on the fire. The roaring flames died down at once, and the city was saved from the disaster. When the people came to thank him and ask him his name, the monk said that his name was made of three horizontal strokes and one vertical stroke. As you know, this is the word *Wang*. Moreover, in our village, when kindhearted people are about to die, they all say that they see Master Wang coming to lead them to Heaven. That is why we know that Master Wang has become an immortal. And that is why we have erected this shrine here in honor and in memory of him."

Liu Ch'ang-sheng sighed and said, "Our master has powers beyond our understanding." The old man who was Wang Ch'ung-yang's cousin said to the disciples, "You have come a long way from Shantung bearing your master to his burial ground, and we thank you for coming to inform us of his passing. We do

大魏村三
老飲舊
昏安礙一
言指迷

子恆

The disciples are shown Wang Ch'ung-yang's shrine at Ta-wei Village. While meditating under a bridge, Hao T'ai-ku receives teachings from a strange man.

not have much to offer except some noodles, rice, and vegetables. Have dinner with us before you return to your homes." The disciples thanked the old man and ate with him that evening. The next morning, word went around that the disciples of the immortal were in the village. One by one the villagers brought food to the old man's house for the disciples. Seeing that they had stirred up attention, the disciples decided that it was time to leave. Liu Ch'ang-sheng consulted with the other disciples, and they decided to leave the remaining money Ma Tan-yang had given them to the old man as a fund with which to maintain their master's shrine. When all was arranged, they said farewell to the old man and left the village.

After walking some ten miles down the road, the disciples rested under a tree. T'an Ch'ang-chen said, "We have fulfilled our master's last wish. We could all return to Shantung, but I do not know what good that will do. We would only use up our brother's money and become a financial burden to him. It is said that all gatherings must disperse. In the Tao, there should be no attachments. If we stay together as a group of wandering monks, people will be suspicious of us and give us no peace. I suggest that from here we should disband and go our separate ways, for we each have our own path to follow." Hao T'ai-ku said, "Brother, you are correct. We should each go our own way now and meet again in the immortal realm."

So Liu Ch'ang-sheng headed southeast, Wang Yü-yang went southwest, T'an Ch'ang-chen went south, and Hao T'ai-ku went east. Ch'iu Ch'ang-ch'un saw that his brothers had taken all the possible branches from the main road. So he decided to tarry in Shensi and selected that region as the place where he would continue his Taoist training.

Walking eastward, Hao T'ai-ku passed by a bridge with seven arches. The foundation of the bridge merged into a group of rock formations that appeared to be dotted by small shallow caves. The river that ran under the bridge was calm and clear. "This is the perfect place for me to meditate," he thought. He entered one of the caves and sat down. At first no one noticed him, but as time went on, some refugees fleeing from famine in the north took shelter in the caves and began to speak of a sage who meditated under the bridge. Curious people from nearby villages came to see this sage, bringing him food. Soon Hao T'ai-ku was surrounded by bowls of rice and noodles and loaves of bread. He could not eat all the food his well-wishers brought, so birds and animals would frequently visit his cave to feed. Children from poor families also began to visit Hao T'ai-ku's cave for food. Soon the cave became a playground for the children. They pretended that he was a buddha and built a small enclosure of stones around him. They bowed to him, chatted with him, and played in the cave. Hao T'ai-ku's foundation in Taoist training was already quite strong by then. Thus he did not mind the children's laughter or the commotion they created. He sought silence in the midst of noise.

One day the children were nowhere to be seen. One of the nearby villages was celebrating a Buddhist festival in honor of Kuan-yin, and the children had gone to the festivities. Hao T'ai-ku walked out of his cave to enjoy the peace and quiet of the surroundings. He noticed a man sitting under one of the arches of the bridge. The man was polishing a stone. Occasionally he would take the polished stone and look at it for a while, then he would resume polishing. He would polish a single stone until it became so thin that it disintegrated; then he would pick up another stone and begin the process all over again. Hao T'ai-ku thought this behavior strange and decided to ask the man the purpose of his activity. He said, "Sir, it appears that you are polishing stones for nothing. Your activity does not seem to lead to any accomplishment. What are you trying to do? Maybe I can help." The man replied, "I am trying to make a mirror by polishing the stone." Hao T'ai-ku said, "People make mirrors by polishing bronze, not stones. If you keep on polishing stones, you will never get what you want." The man laughed and said, "You are telling me that if I stubbornly sit here and polish my stones, I shall never make a mirror! What about you? Do you think that by sitting here stubbornly in the cave you can become an immortal?" Hao T'ai-ku realized what the man was trying to teach him by his actions. But as he was about to ask this strange man for more instructions, the man suddenly disappeared. Hao

T'ai-ku said to himself, "The sage was right. Stubbornly sitting here all the time is 'dead sitting.' " He went back into the cave, collected his belongings, and left the area.

After parting from the other disciples, T'an Ch'ang-chen took the road south. One night as he was nearing a town he could not find any abandoned shrines or houses in which to take shelter. Looking around, he suddenly saw a large mansion with many buildings within its walls. He knocked on the front door to ask for shelter. The master of the mansion was a man name Ku Tsu-ting. In his youth he had been interested in the teachings of the Tao, but unfortunately he had been taken advantage of by many self-proclaimed Taoist masters who were actually swindlers. As a result he developed an adversity toward any kind of religious teaching and shunned the company of monks as well as anyone who had the slightest bent toward spirituality. When Ku Tsu-ting opened the door and saw a Taoist monk, he said bluntly to T'an Ch'ang-chen, "My relationship with Taoism has ended. My house has no place for Buddhist and Taoist monks. Please go away." T'an Ch'ang-chen saw that Ku Tsu-ting was an honest and sincere man and that the illusions he had built around himself could be dissolved. He decided that he would speak with this man and lead him back to the path of the Tao.

17

T'an Ch'ang=chen was about to explain to Ku Tsu-ting that not all self-professed Taoists are dishonest persons when Ku Tsu-ting said, "Taoist monk, you need say nothing more. I've heard what you are about to say from many people. And they cheated me. You are all hypocrites." The door was shut in T'an Ch'ang-chen's face. T'an Ch'ang-chen was not discouraged. He wanted to show the master of the house that there are people who sincerely seek the Tao. Seeing that it was late into the night, he decided to sit in front of the Ku mansion to meditate. Around midnight, the door opened and Ku Tsu-ting's servants poured a bucket of cold water on him. T'an Ch'ang-chen moved to an area across the road. The night turned cold and it began to snow. The storm intensified and by dawn, there was a foot of snow on the ground except for a small area around T'an Ch'ang-chen.

When Ku Tsu-ting's servants opened the door and saw the melted spot around T'an Ch'ang-chen, they were astonished and reported what they saw to their master. Ku Tsu-ting came out and walked to where T'an Ch'ang-chen was sitting. Not only was the snow around the Taoist monk melted, but a heat was felt radiating from his body. Ku Tsu-ting realized that T'an Ch'ang-chen was no fraud. Bowing respectfully he said, "Sir, you are a geniune Taoist master. Forgive my rudeness to you last night. It is just that I have met so many fraudulent Taoist practitioners that I am disillusioned. People like you are rare. I would be honored if you would stay at my home and be my teacher. If you are willing, tomorrow I shall be initiated as your disciple." T'an Ch'ang-chen had wanted to lead Ku Tsu-ting back into the path of the Tao and saw this to be an excellent opportunity. So he said, "Very well, I shall accept you as a student."

That very day Ku Tsu-ting ordered the servants to clean out a quiet room in the mansion for T'an Ch'ang-chen. He also assigned a servant to attend to T'an Ch'ang-chen's needs. As T'an Ch'ang-chen settled into the Ku mansion, he discovered that Ku Tsu-ting was not ready to adopt the rigorous training demanded by Taoist practice. He was contented simply to serve his master, knowing that he would reap the rewards for performing a good deed. After staying at the Ku mansion for a month, T'an Ch'ang-chen decided to leave. But time after time Ku Tsu-ting begged him stay.

Seeing that leaving the Ku mansion was going to be a difficult affair, T'an Ch'ang-chen thought of a plan. The next morning, when the servant girl brought breakfast to his room, T'an Ch'ang-chen pretended to flirt with her. Appalled, the servant reported T'an Ch'ang-chen's behavior to her master. Not only did Ku Tsu-ting not believe the servant, but he reprimanded her for lying. "Master T'an is an honorable man. He would not do such disgraceful things." A few days later, Ku Tsu-ting was in the living room when he heard noises in the hallway. When he went to investigate what was happening, he saw T'an Ch'ang-chen making bold advances to the servant girl. Ku Tsu-ting did not know what to do. He had invited T'an Ch'ang-chen to live at his home, and even when the Taoist monk wanted to leave he had begged him to stay. Besides, he had been formally initiated as a disciple of T'an Ch'ang-chen; courtesy and propriety forbade him to order his teacher to leave. So he left a note to T'an Ch'ang-chen alluding to his disgraceful actions and told the servants not to stop T'an Ch'ang-chen if the monk decided to leave.

When T'an Ch'ang-chen read Ku Tsu-ting's note, he wrote a response, telling his student that his behavior toward the servant girl had been a plan of escape from the Ku mansion. That day when T'an Ch'ang-chen walked out of the front door of the Ku mansion, no one stopped him. When Ku Tsu-ting found T'an Ch'ang-chen's note and realized the truth behind his master's actions, it was too late. By then T'an Ch'ang-chen had vanished.

After parting with his brothers, Wang Yü-yang journeyed on the southwest road and came to a small town nestled in the rural region of Fang County. In this town lived a wealthy man who had retired from government service after becoming disillusioned with politics and power. His name was Yao Chung-kao, and he had built himself a comfortable home in rustic surroundings.

戯喜紅定計脱身難渾然富真盤道

子桓

T'an Ch'ang-chen pretends to flirt with the servant girl in a
plan to escape from the Ku mansion.

Delighting in simple living, he spent much of his time tending his flower gardens and reading Buddhist and Taoist scriptures. He also actively sought people with spiritual interests and entertained many Buddhist and Taoist wandering monks. In that same town was a small Taoist temple called the Immortals' Meeting Place. The temple's abbot was a Taoist priest who had more skill in entertaining visitors than interpreting the scriptures. Since many wandering monks took shelter in the temple, Yao Chung-kao requested that the abbot notify him of any interesting monks who were staying there. A few weeks before Wang Yü-yang's arrival, an odd-looking man appeared at the temple gates. He was neither Buddhist nor Taoist but claimed to have extraordinary powers. He claimed to be ninety-six years old. He claimed to have learned from the Taoist master Chang San-feng and to have communicated with Immortal Lü Tung-pin. He also said that Bodhidharma had transmitted teachings to him in a dream. When the abbot asked him his name, he replied, "My name is Immortal Hun Yüan [meaning 'the undifferentiated original one']." When the abbot told Yao Chung-kao about this strange visitor, Yao Chung-kao at once invited this immortal Hun Yüan to his home.

The first thing Hun Yüan said to Yao Chung-kao was, "The Buddhists are sex-repressed and sex-starved maniacs. The Taoists are stealers of internal energy. If you go with either of those philosophies you will not be able to attain enlightenment. My way, on the other hand, is the rightful path to enlightenment. Look at me. I have achieved enlightenment. I am the one who can teach you. Those Buddhists and Taoists are all frauds." Yao Chung-kao was taken in by Hun Yüan's strange appearance and bold assertiveness. He asked Hun Yüan to be his teacher and invited him to stay at his home. As time went on Hun Yüan became more and more outspoken against Buddhism and Taoism. He would attract crowds in the market place and even gave oratory speeches in front of the temple denouncing Taoism. The abbot and the resident monks became annoyed by his diatribes, but none of them had the knowledge or skill to debate with him. As if events had been arranged from Heaven, Wang Yü-yang arrived at the temple asking for shelter and food.

When the abbot saw Wang Yü-yang he knew that this was a

person advanced in Taoist training. In contrast to the sallow complexion of "Immortal" Hun Yüan, Wang Yü-yang's cheeks were rosy and his bearing robust. His composure was calm, and his eyes reflected an unusual brightness. The abbot knew that if there was anyone who could reveal the falsehood of Hun Yüan, this would be the man. Several times the abbot thought about asking Wang Yü-yang to debate with Hun Yüan, but he was afraid that Wang Yü-yang would refuse. Finally he came up with a plan to arrange a meeting between the two men. The morning after Wang Yü-yang's arrival the abbot said to him, "Master, there is a person of great learning and power living in the Yao mansion, and the master of the house delights in meeting Taoist monks. Perhaps you might be interested in meeting both of them." Not knowing the plot, Wang Yü-yang agreed.

They arrived at the Yao mansion and announced themselves, and a servant led them into the living room. Yao Chung-kao welcomed them and was about to engage in a conversation with Wang Yü-yang when Hun Yüan entered the living room. He walked right in front of Yao Chung-kao, brushed past Wang Yü-yang rudely, and sat down in the seat of honor reserved for persons of high rank. The abbot turned to Wang Yü-yang and said, "He is the man of learning and power that I was referring to." Wang Yü-yang walked up to Hun Yüan and offered his greetings respectfully. Hun Yüan nodded and said in a haughty voice, "You monk, are you married or not?" Wang Yü-yang replied, "I was married, but I have left my family." Hun Yüan laughed and said, "You ignorant one. You call yourself a Taoist monk, and you don't even know the meaning of my question. Let me instruct you then. When I asked you if you were married or not, in Taoist terminology this meant whether you have balanced you *yin* and *yang* energies. If you don't even know this, how can you understand more complex concepts such as 'ten months of pregnancy'?" Wang Yü-yang was not affected by Hun Yüan's remarks. Calmly and quietly he said, "Sir, you talk of balancing the *yin* and *yang* energies. What does that mean? You talk of the 'ten months of pregnancy.' What is being conceived in the womb?" Hun Yüan was stunned by these questions. He did not know the answers, so he blurted out, "The mystery of the heavens cannot be revealed. I will not answer your questions." Seeing that Hun Yüan had given a forced answer to cover his ignorance, the abbot said to Wang Yü-yang, "Friend, why don't you explain your questions to him? It seems that he does not understand what you are saying."

18

Hun Yüan was becoming irritated. The abbot chuckled to himself, "Now you get a dose of your own medicine." Wang Yü-yang then said to Hun Yüan, "Sir, you do not have to answer me if you feel that your answers may anger the gods in Heaven. If you will permit, I shall try to expound the answer, and people can judge whether I am correct or not."

Wang Yü-yang then said, "The true *yin* and *yang* energies reside in internal organs in our body. The true *yang* is stored in the liver and the true *yin* in the lungs. The liver belongs to the element wood. It is the dwelling place of the spirit. The lungs belong to the element metal. It is the dwelling place of the soul. Metal is said to be the daughter of Tui ("lake"), the western house of the pa-kua. Wood is said to be the son of Chen ("thunder"), the eastern house of the pa-kua. That is why it is said that wood thrives in the east and metal takes life in the west. This is the meaning of the symbolism of the marriage between the son of the east and the daughter of the west. When the couple is in unison, then soul and spirit are not separated from each other. When Master Hun Yüan asked me if I was married or not, he was asking me whether the Yellow Woman, the go-between, had introduced the *yin* and *yang* energies to each other. The copulation of the *yin* and *yang* energies produces the seed that is carried in the womb for ten months. The seed is the Golden Pill formed from the purified vital energy in the body. The term "ten months of pregnancy" is used to describe the state of body while the spirit is forming. Thus, it is said that the spirit is the son of the vital energy and vital energy is the mother of the spirit. When the spirit is fully formed, it emerges from the body like a newborn baby. The alchemical work is now complete, and one can age with the sun and moon and merge with the Heaven and earth."

Yao Chung-kao clapped his hands and praised Wang Yü-yang's scholarship. Hun Yüan was now beginning to fear that Yao Chung-kao might abandon him and seek advice from Wang Yü-yang instead. He said, "Wang Yü-yang, you may know how to talk eloquently, but the real test lies in one's actions. If you dare, we shall have a competition to see who can sit and meditate longest. I can sit for three days straight without touching food and water. Let us see if you can do it." Wang Yü-yang smiled and said, "My foundation is shallow. I cannot sit very long. But if it is a question of two or three days I think I shall be able to oblige."

Hun Yüan and Wang Yü-yang each sat on meditation cushions in Yao Chung-kao's living room. They sat through the first day without moving, but on the second day Hun Yüan became uncomfortable. To begin with, his mind was already full of anger and irritation. The competition had become a matter of life and death to him, and he badly wanted to defeat Wang Yü-yang. As a result, his mind wandered and could not keep still. He started feeling thirst and hunger and found that he could not keep awake. By the middle of the second day, Hun Yüan could not sit longer. He got up, ate some food, drank some water, and fell asleep. Wang Yü-yang sat through the third day and at sunset he slowly uncrossed his legs and got up. He felt invigorated and full of energy. Yao Chung-kao and the abbot praised Wang Yü-yang endlessly. Even Hun Yüan admitted that Wang Yü-yang's abilities surpassed his own by far. Wang Yü-yang said humbly, "Master Hun Yüan's foundation is not weak. Because of his old age, his body does not have the strength to maintain the same posture for a long period of time. I won because I am younger and my body is more flexible." Hun Yüan heard these words and was ashamed. He said to Wang Yü-yang, "Master, you are a truly enlightened being. I thought I had attained enlightenment, but I was wrong. Now I know that there is much to learn." Seeing Hun Yüan's sincerity, Wang Yü-yang gave him some basic instructions in sitting meditation.

Wang Yü-yang stayed at the Yao mansion for two days. On the third day he told Yao Chung-kao that he had some business to do at the temple in town, but after leaving Yao's house he never returned. When the abbot told Yao Chung-kao that Wang Yü-yang had left town, Yao Chung-kao sighed and said, "Maybe the time has not yet come for me to receive the teachings of the Tao from a master."

王玉陽以真服
假譚長真
說古證
今
子桓

Wang Yü-yang wins over imposter Hun Yüan. Liu Ch'ang-
sheng visits the palace of the Empress of Heaven and falls into
temptation.

103

Liu Ch'ang-sheng journeyed south and then east. He arrived at T'ai Shan, a group of mountains on the eastern coast, and there he lived as a hermit for three years. One day he felt that his cultivation of the Golden Pill was complete, so he made an astral journey to the palace of the Empress of Heaven. The Empress and her court ladies were seated under a canopy surrounded by many-colored clouds. When Liu Ch'ang-sheng saw the beauty of the ladies he could not resist peeking at them out of the corner of his eye. His behavior was noticed by the Empress, who said, "Liu Ch'ang-sheng, why are you looking at my attendants?" Liu Ch'ang-sheng fell down on his face. Trembling, he asked the Empress for forgiveness. "Your majesty, I saw the beauty of the ladies and could not hide my admiration. I had no other intentions." The Empress replied, "You still have a trace of sexual desire in you. Don't you know that even though your Golden Pill may be fully developed, if you cannot empty your mind of sexual craving, you will never be able to ascend to the highest heavens. Because your mind is not pure, you must return to the earthly realm and continue to cultivate yourself." The Empress then ordered the door guards of the gates of Heaven to escort Liu Ch'ang-sheng from the palace. At the door of the palace, the guards gave Liu Ch'ang-sheng a push, and Liu Ch'ang-sheng fell back into the earthly realm. The fall woke him up, and he realized that his visit to the palace of the Empress of Heaven had been a dream. "Thank goodness this was only a dream. My master warned me that my sexual desires were not completely dissolved. Now the omens have come to tell me to confront this problem. I must leave the mountains and find someone to instruct me."

Liu Ch'ang-sheng left T'ai Shan. After traveling for three days, he met T'an Ch'ang-chen on the road. The two brothers greeted each other and related what they had experienced. When T'an Ch'ang-chen heard Liu Ch'ang-sheng's description of his dream and learned of his search for a teacher to advise him, T'an Ch'ang-chen said, "Let me tell you a story." They sat down under a tree, and T'an Ch'ang-chen said, "Once there was a man named Hu Hsiang-yang. In his youth he was a skilled archer and enjoyed hunting. One day his arrow pierced a fawn. The fawn ran away with the arrow lodged in its body. Hu Hsiang-yang gathered his servants and tracked the fawn to a hidden valley. There he saw the fawn lying on the ground and the mother deer standing next to it licking the wound. As the men approached, the mother deer did not run but stood in front of the fawn. In the end both mother and fawn were captured. The fawn died of its wounds on the way back to Hu Hsiang-yang's village. The mother deer died that night in captivity. When the animals were skinned for preparation of the meat, Hu Hsiang-yang found that the internal organs of the mother deer had split open. Seeing that the mother's grief for her young caused such traumatic consequences, Hu Hsiang-yang was moved. That day he broke his bow and arrows and made an oath that he would not kill a living thing for the rest of his life. He left his home, met a Taoist sage, and went with him into the mountains.

"Years later, after Hu Hsiang-yang had attained enlightenment, he returned to teach and had more than one hundred students. One day Hsiang-yang asked his students whether they had severed their attachments to worldly desires. All his students claimed to have done so. Hu Hsiang-yang then said to them, 'I shall give you a test. If you pass this test then I shall give you advanced instructions in internal alchemy. This is the test: each of you should take a plank of wood measuring four feet by two feet. Place it on your bed tonight and sleep beside it. Bring your plank with you when you report to me the next morning.' The students went away thinking that they would all pass such an easy test with flying colors. That night each student went to sleep lying beside a wooden plank. In the middle of the night, as each one turned toward the plank, he felt something warm and soft. Groping around, he felt the body of a naked young woman. The students' sexual fires were aroused at once, and their generative energy drained out of their bodies. Each one's heart was full of desire for the body beside him, and even in sleep he embraced it.

"On awakening the next morning, the students saw that they were hugging the wooden planks. They sat up bewildered, but from outside the dormitory the teacher's bell was heard, summoning them to the instruction hall. The students hurriedly filed into the hall with their planks. Hu Hsiang-yang ordered each of them to show him the wooden plank. The first student on the line was a man seventy-six years of age. Hu Hsiang-yang looked at him and said, 'At your age you still cling to sexual desires.' The old man said, 'Sir, how do you know that I have not severed my ties to sexual craving?' Hu Hsiang-yang replied, 'Look at your plank. There are stains of your semen on it. Your sexual desires were roused when you felt a naked body next to you and with that your generative energy was drained.' The man hung his head in shame and walked to the back of the room. Hu Hsiang-yang then said, 'If there is anyone whose plank has no stain of seminal fluid on it, let him step up.' There was a long silence. The students did not dare to step forward, because when they examined their planks they found them to be stained with their involuntary emissions.

"Only one person in the middle of the line stepped forward to present his plank to the master. Hu Hsiang-yang said, 'The desire for sex is strong for the typical person. You seemed to have tamed this desire. How did you manage to do it?' The man replied, 'Sir, I learned abstinence by overexposure.' Hu Hsiang-yang said, 'How so?' The student said, 'Most people know that their desires will ultimately lead to harm. However, they do not acknowledge the danger until they have tasted it. Once one has experienced the adverse consequences of sexual craving then one will avoid it like the plague. As time goes on, the body strengthens itself through abstinence, and the craving stops long after the fear is gone. When I was an adolescent I could not control my sexual craving. I frequented the brothels and lay with a woman every night. As a result, after a few years my body was drained of energy and my mind was stripped of clarity. I almost died because I could not resist the temptation of sex. After that, I learned my lesson. I thought about my past experiences and saw that I had not really been happy when I was in the brothels. Ladies come and go. I made love to them, but I did not know who they were and they did not care who I was. This went on continually, just as day follows night, and I began to see the emptiness of sexual craving. Sir, I am no longer attached to sexual desire because I have experienced it, have suffered the consequences of my indulgence, and have seen the emptiness in the endless repetition of lovemaking.' Hu Hsiang-yang nodded his head and said to him, 'You are the only student who is ready to receive the advanced teachings. The rest of the people need more work in preparing their foundations.' It was said that the student received the transmission of the teachings of the Tao from Hu Hsiang-yang and eventually attained enlightenment." T'an Ch'ang-chen finished his story and added, "Thus the sages have said that in order to dissolve a desire one must see its emptiness."

Liu Ch'ang-sheng said, "Brother, your story has inspired me. The brothels will be the place of my training. I shall look on the activities there until I see the emptiness in them." T'an Ch'ang-chen said, "We are nearing the birthplace of Lao-tzu. Let us visit the shrine first, and then we can continue on our separate ways." Liu Ch'ang-sheng consented. They had not walked far when they met Wang Yü-yang. Wang Yü-yang greeted them and related his experiences at the Yao mansion to them. Liu Ch'ang-sheng remarked, "It looks as though that imposter Hun Yüan got some instructions for nothing." Wang Yü-yang said, "Hun Yüan slandered the Tao. If I had not engaged in a competition with him in meditation, he would still be making speeches against Taoism." T'an Ch'ang-chen said, "Brother, we do not train to compete. And what we have learned should not be used as a show for others." The three disciples continued to chat as they walked along. Suddenly they heard a voice from behind calling to them to stop and wait. They looked back and saw Hao T'ai-ku hurrying down the road toward them.

19

The four disciples arrived at Lao-tzu's birthplace. There they saw a small shrine with an octagonal enclosure surrounded by nine wells. Inside the shrine was a stone inscribed with the legend concerning Lao-tzu's birth. According to legend, during the time of the Shang dynasty (1766–1121 B.C.E.) there was a village in Fu County whose inhabitants were masters of divination. These villagers lived the simple life of recluses and did not seek fame and fortune in politics or military deeds. Among the villagers was a young woman of nineteen who was known for her intelligence and wisdom. Once summer day she was resting under a tree that had borne unusually large red fruits that year. The day was hot, so the young woman ate a fruit to quench her thirst. The fruit she picked was bright and shiny and looked like no ordinary fruit. A few days after she ate the fruit, the girl found herself pregnant. When the villagers consulted the oracles it was revealed to them that a great sage was to be born in the region. However, the oracle also told them to pick a year, month, day, and hour for the sage to be born, for it was important for the heavenly bodies to be in the most favorable celestial positions to herald the birth of the sage. The villagers calculated the celestial positions of the stars again and again, but they could not find an appropriate date until eighty-one years had passed since the young woman's conception. By now the woman was over one hundred years old, but during the time she bore the fetus she was immune to heat and cold, did not feel hunger or thirst, and was not inflicted with illness.

It was said that on the appointed day Lao-tzu tumbled out of his earthly mother's belly, and as he hit the ground a clap of thunder rang through the sky. His hair was white, and he could walk and talk the moment he was born. He walked forward seven steps, walked back three steps, and said in a loud voice, "Heaven and earth will acknowledge me as the Ancient One." At once music was heard from the heavens and fragrant flowers flew through the air. Fairies danced on rainbow-colored clouds, and nine dragons showered Lao-tzu with water. It is said that as the waters of the dragons hit the ground nine wells sprouted up, and the water of those nine wells had never dried up even in times of drought. Lao-tzu took the family name Li because he took life from the fruit of the li tree. Because he was born white-haired, he was known as the Lao-tzu, meaning "the old sage."

Moved by the surrounding scenery and the legend of Lao-tzu's birth, the disciples said to each other, "We who have cultivated the Tao all these years owe our teachings to the Ancient One. Let us each speak a few lines of poetry in honor of Lao-tzu and reveal what we have learned during all these years."

Hao T'ai-ku was first to recite his lines. "The sword of wisdom hangs high among the cold north stars. The hands of the monsters of illusion are bound tight. On the meditation cushion during the midnight hour, the dragon and the tiger copulate when the Pill circulates nine times to return to the Source." Next, Wang Yü-yang recited: "Viewing the ancient ways from the immortal realm, the heat and cold are gathered. In the critical hours of the alchemical process, when Golden Raven and Jade Rabbit meet, the dragon will rumble and the tiger will roar." When T'an Ch'ang-chen's turn came he recited, "The ways of the Tao have no limits. The hand of monsters and ghosts are cold when they strike. If you want to transcend the mortal to become immortal, you must strike through the barriers of illusion with an iron fist. Then in the stove and cauldron the roar of the dragon and tiger can be heard." Lastly, Liu Ch'ang-sheng recited, "That which is spoken chills the heart. The intelligent are deceived by intelligence and become fools. What is this talk about the immortal dragon and tiger?"

When the disciples had thus revealed to each other their understanding of the Tao, Wang Yü-yang said to Liu Ch'ang-sheng, "Brother, the three of us spoke of progress and immanent success in the alchemical work. You alone alluded to failure. Why do you let negative attitudes dominate you thinking?" T'an Ch'ang-chen said to Wang Yü-yang, "There is wisdom in knowing what chills the heart and in knowing the pitfalls of intelligence. Although the mystery of the Tao is not explicitly described, that mystery is embedded in the meanings of the words.

論玄機四言

契妙道
開山洞一人
獨勤勞

子樞

The disciples visit the birthplace of Lao-tzu. Hao T'ai-ku
excavates grottoes in the cliffs of Hua Shan.

The references to success and failure are in your mind and not in his words." Hao T'ai-ku said to T'an Ch'ang-chen, "Brother, you have not revealed all." T'an Ch'ang-chen laughed and said, "That is right. Brother Liu Ch'ang-sheng had a dream in which he met with the Empress of Heaven. He could not control his admiration for the beauty of the court ladies, and he looked at them from the corner of his eye. The Empress was angry with him and told him to return to the earthly realm to dissolve his remaining desires. I recounted a story about the sage Hu Hsiang-yang, and Liu Ch'ang-sheng came up with the idea that he should go to the brothels to cultivate his heart and empty it of sexual desires." Wang Yü-yang said, "Why does he need to go to the brothels? Is it not enough to cultivate the attitude that sees no evil and hears no evils?" Hao T'ai-ku added, "Forget yourself, forget others, and all desires will dissolve." Liu Ch'ang-sheng said, "Brothers, you offer good advice. But the methods of cultivation that you speak of are only appropriate for those who have strong foundations. I am afraid I would not be able to change my attitude by will. I need to expose myself to the activities in the brothels so that I can see through the illusions of sexual attractions and desire." Wang Yü-yang and Hao T'ai-ku said, "Many people have sought ways to dissolve sexual desire, but we have never heard that going to the brothels was a method." T'an Ch'ang-chen said, "Methods are the inventions of people. The intelligent will come up with a way that will work best for them. The stubborn will stick to existing methods even though they are inappropriate. Let us not discuss this matter any longer. Brother Liu Ch'ang-sheng has made up his mind. We shall rest here tonight, and tomorrow each of us shall continue on his way."

The next day the disciples said farewell to one another and parted. Hao T'ai-ku continued westward to Shensi. He saw the majestic peaks of Hua Shan, the interplay of sunlight and shadows on the cliffs, and said, "When I was carrying the bier of the master, my back was bent and I was unable to look on the wonder of the mountains. Now I know why generations of Taoists attained immortality in these peaks." As Hao T'ai-ku explored the mountains of Hua Shan he was especially taken by a vertical slab of rock face that pointed up to the sky like a palm. He suddenly remembered Wang Ch'ung-yang's final words to him: "Hao T'ai-ku, you will wander east and west but will not attain the Tao until you have reached the top of the cliff-edged mountains." Hao T'ai-ku climbed to the top of the palm-shaped mountain and decided to dig a cave where he could meditate in peace. He spent much time and effort in excavating a hole large enough for one person to sit cross-legged in, but on the day he finished a Taoist hermit arrived and asked Hao T'ai-ku if he could spare him the cave. Before Hao T'ai-ku could answer the man stepped inside the hollow and sat down. Hao T'ai-ku was by nature a kind and generous person, so he picked up his belongings and went to another isolated region to excavate another cave. Scarecly had he finished digging his cave when another Taoist hermit arrived and said to him, "Brother in the Tao, can you spare me your cave so that I can meditate in peace? I am old, and I do not have much time." Hao T'ai-ku replied, "You can have the cave, and may you achieve enlightenment soon."

Over the next ten years Hao T'ai-ku excavated seventy-two caves among the cliffs of Hua Shan. Each time just as he was about to settle inside his cave someone arrived asking for it, and seventy-two times Hao T'ai-ku gave up what he had dug with hard labor. Finally, Hao T'ai-ku saw a ledge halfway down a precarious cliff. He said to himself, "If I went down to the ledge and hollowed out part of the wall behind it, I would be able to meditate there without any people finding me." So he went to the nearest village and bought some ropes. On the way back to Hua Shan he found a man who begged Hao T'ai-ku to accept him as a disciple. Seeing the man's sincerity, Hao T'ai-ku said, "Follow me to Hua Shan." Teacher and disciple arrived at the cliff where the ledge stood. Hao T'ai-ku tied one end of the rope to a tree and climbed down to the ledge. There he began to hollow out a small cave sufficient for one person to sit in. The disciple prepared meals for him once a day, lowering a food basket down to the ledge. Hao T'ai-ku would descend to the ledge early in the morning and climb back up at sunset. This went on for months. When the disciple saw that his teacher did nothing but dig, he became impatient. He said to himself, "I became his disciple so that I could learn the arts of the Tao and become immortal. It has been months since I followed him, and I have not learned anything. All I do is prepare meals and gather firewood. I am never going to receive any instructions from my teacher. He simply wants me to cook for him and tend to his needs."

One morning, the disciple followed Hao T'ai-ku to the edge of the cliff. As usual, Hao T'ai-ku tied one end of the rope to a tree and lowered himself down to the ledge. While his teacher was hanging onto the rope, the disciple took his axe and hacked at the rope until it broke. He hoped that Hao T'ai-ku would be killed as he fell thousands of feet down the mountain.

The following day the disciple packed up his belongings and headed down the mountain. Halfway down the slopes he saw a man climbing nimbly up the trail. The man looked like his teacher, and when they came within talking distance the disciple's mouth dropped open. The man was indeed his teacher, Hao T'ai-ku. He blurted out, "Sir, where have you been?" Hao T'ai-ku laughed good-naturedly and said, "This morning I discovered that some of my digging tools needed sharpening, so I decided to head for the nearest village to ask the blacksmith to sharpen them for me. Well, why are you here? You wre supposed to wait for me up by the cliff." The disciple stammered, "Sir, I waited for you all morning until noon. When I could not find you I decided to come down the mountain to look for you." Hao T'ai-ku said, "That was very kind of you. I am so glad to meet you here. See, the sun is already setting. We would not be able to make it up to the cliff today. It is a good thing that you have brought all the cooking utensils. How considerate of you! Let us camp here for the night and make dinner." That night, as he was trying to sleep, the disciple thought to himself, "This is strange indeed. Hao T'ai-ku must have fallen thousands of feet when the rope was cut. No mortal could have survived that kind of a fall. Besides, he was on top of the mountain yesterday and now, only one day later, he has been to the village and was halfway up the mountain. He must have known that someone cut his rope, but he acted as if nothing had happened. Surely this man must be an immortal. If I left him I would lose my chance of becoming an immortal."

Next morning, Hao T'ai-ku and his disciple continued up the mountain and arrived at the cliff, where the severed rope was still tied to the tree. The disciple ventured to say, "Sir, the rope is broken. How can you get down to the ledge?" Hao T'ai-ku replied, "That is not a problem. If there is no rope, I'll just jump down." With that Hao T'ai-ku leapt over the edge of the cliff and disappeared.

20

Liu Ch'ang-sheng arrived in the Su-hang region, an area in southern China. The Su-hang region was known for producing beautiful women, and its brothels had courtesans who were not only beautiful but also talented in music, painting, and poetry. On the way into town, Liu Ch'ang-sheng picked up some stones and turned them into gold pieces. He exchanged his monkish garb for the fine array of a rich merchant and walked into one of the most exquisite brothels in the town. Liu Ch'ang-sheng sought out the proprietess of the brothel and said to her, "My name is Ch'ang Sheng-tzu. I am a jewel merchant from the north. I have heard that your house has the most beautiful ladies in the area. I would like to have the company of one who can play the lute, make poetry, and converse in intelligent subjects." The proprietess, hearing that Liu Ch'ang-sheng was a jewel merchant, said, "Sir, that would not be difficult. I shall introduce you to Madam Yü. She excels in dancing, music, poetry, painting, and chess, and she is beautiful and gentle." She led Liu Ch'ang-sheng to Madam Yü's room and said, "Sir, you are welcome to stay here as long as you wish. If you have any needs, just ring for the servant."

Madam Yü looked at Liu Ch'ang-sheng and saw that he was not only handsome but had a regal bearing that set him apart from her other customers. Whereas her other customers desired her body and often made violent sexual approaches to her, this man respected her and spoke to her gently, treating her not as a sexual object but as a friend. Liu Ch'ang-sheng conducted himself according to what Wang Ch'ung-yang had taught him: "View everything before you with calmness. True stillness is when a landslide passes before you and you are not disturbed." Thus, Liu Ch'ang-sheng treated the beautiful woman before him as an empty form. His heart was not moved, and therefore his body did not desire her. Because his intentions were pure, his senses did not attach themselves onto the "attractions" in front of him. Liu Ch'ang-sheng and Madam Yü enjoyed each other's company as friends. They ate together. They played music together, and they even slept together in the same bed, but as far as Liu Ch'ang-sheng was concerned he was sleeping beside a plank of wood. All this time Liu Ch'ang-sheng told his eyes to look but not see Madam Yü's beauty, his ears to listen but not hear her seductive voice. Anybody looking at their actions would see two people playing with each other like children.

When the other ladies in the brothel heard of Liu Ch'ang-sheng's strange relationship with Madam Yü, they were curious and asked that they be allowed to attend Liu Ch'ang-sheng as well. The proprietess, who was kept happy by Liu Ch'ang-sheng's seemingly endless supply of gold pieces, was too eager to please her rich customer to care about Liu Ch'ang-sheng's unconventional sexual behavior. Thus Liu Ch'ang-sheng was often accompanied by five or six ladies who were continually amused by his lack of sexual interest toward them and the friendly and understanding way in which he treated them, not as objects for pleasure but as intelligent human beings.

One day the ladies had bought some flowers for Liu Ch'ang-sheng and persuaded him to dress up as a woman. Liu Ch'ang-sheng laughed and consented. Just as the ladies were beginning to dress him in woman's clothing and put flowers in his hair, the door of the room opened and a bearded, long-haired monk stepped in. The monk had bushy eyebrows and the complexion and features of one from the lands far to the west over the great mountains. This monk was none other than Bodhidharma, the great patriarch of Buddhism, who was wandering through China visiting the Buddhist monasteries. He was passing through the Su-hang region when he saw a purple cloud hovering over the brothel where Liu Ch'ang-sheng was staying. Knowing that the purple cloud signified the presence of an immortal, Bodhidharma decided to seek out this enlightened person.

When Bodhidharma burst into the room the ladies were shocked by his foreign appearance, and they hurriedly ran behind Liu Ch'ang-sheng for protection. When Liu Ch'ang-sheng saw Bodhidharma he knew that this was an enlightened person, a bodhisattva who had dissolved all attachments to craving and desire. He rose from his seat and respectfully asked Bodhidharma

煉色相
烟花
混跡
說妙偈
道念
純真
于桓

*Liu Ch'ang-sheng tames his sexual desires by living in the
brothel.*

to have tea with him. There was no hot water to make fresh tea, so Liu Ch'ang-sheng took a pot of cold water and pressed it against his lower *tan-t'ien*. After a while, the water in the pot started to boil. Liu Ch'ang-sheng put some tea leaves in the hot water and presented the tea to Bodhidharma. The ladies who were hiding behind Liu Ch'ang-sheng were astonished. They had never before seen someone heat up water with his body. Seeing their bewilderment, Liu Ch'ang-sheng said to them, "Heating water with my belly is nothing extraordinary. See, my belly can also bake hotcakes." Liu Ch'ang-sheng took a stack of hotcakes and pressed them against his *tan-t'ien*. He worked up the fires in his body, and in a few seconds the cakes were baked. While the ladies marveled, Bodhidharma acted as if nothing out of the ordinary had happened. For Bodhidharma was an enlightened being. He did not feel challenged by the Taoist, nor did he feel that he himself needed to demonstrate some of his abilities. On the contrary, Bodhidharma said good-naturedly, "Your method of cooking is so wonderful! Maybe someday we'll get together and you can teach me." Bodhidharma finished his tea and bid farewell to Liu Ch'ang-sheng. As he was about to leave the room, Bodhidharma said, "You who already know the east road where you came from, why not take the west road and leave? Before your original nature becomes contaminated, you should speedily return home." Liu Ch'ang-sheng replied, "In emptiness there is no direction and there is no coming and going. How can an original nature that is pure become contaminated? My body does not have a master. Where should it find its home?" Hearing these words, Bodhidharma knew that they could have been uttered only by an enlightened man. Respectfully he bowed to Liu Ch'ang-sheng and left.

Liu Ch'ang-sheng had been staying at the brothel for over a year when Wang Yü-yang came through the Su-hang region on his way south. Eager to find out how his brother was doing, Wang Yü-yang decided to find Liu Ch'ang-sheng. When he arrived at the brothel where Liu Ch'ang-sheng was staying, the ladies welcomed him and said, "Sir, are you looking for the man who can cook cakes on his belly?" Wang Yü-yang laughed and said, "Yes, but how do you know?" The ladies replied, "A while ago a Buddhist monk visited our guest. Since you are also a monk, you must be looking for Ch'ang Sheng-tzu as well." They led Wang Yü-yang to the guest rooms were Liu Ch'ang-sheng was staying. Wang Yü-yang heard laughing and jesting voices from one of the rooms and recognized that one of the voices belonged to his brother. He walked up quietly to an open window and used his internal energy to fan the candle flames, lighting up the room so that the flames roared up like a firestorm. The women screamed in horror, but Liu Ch'ang-sheng laughed mildly and said, "Do not be afraid. It is only the monsters playing tricks on me." Wang Yü-yang opened the door, smiled and said, "No, I am playing tricks on the monsters." Liu Ch'ang-sheng said, "If you say I am a monster I shall not argue with you. However, it is monstrous to use fire to harm people." Wang Yü-yang was about to formulate a rebuttal when Liu Ch'ang-sheng said, "Brother, hurry and leave. You must go immediately to the south. There is someone waiting for you to accompany him to the immortal realm." As Wang Yü-yang turned to leave, he said to Liu Ch'ang-sheng, "Brother, when are you planning to leave this place?" Liu Ch'ang-sheng replied, "I shall leave when I leave." Wang Yü-yang nodded, bowed, and left.

On the road south Wang Yü-yang met T'an Chang-chen. Together they decided to head for the mountains in the southwest to spend some time in solitude and meditation. It is said that in the cloud-covered peaks of the southwest region of China, Wang Yü-yang and T'an Ch'ang-chen attained the Tao and became immortal. As for Liu Ch'ang-sheng, he left the brothel soon after Wang Yü-yang's visit. His sexual desires completely dissolved, he was now ready to leave the mortal realm. Liu Ch'ang-sheng retreated into the mountains near the eastern coast and, after three years of meditation, became immortal and ascended into the heavens. Hao T'ai-ku attained immortality on the cliffs of Hua Shan, shedding his mortal shell when he leapt off the cliff of the palm-shaped mountain.

21

$Sun\ Pu\text{-}erh$ lived in the city of Loyang for twelve years. She attained the Tao and acquired powerful magical abilities. One day she said to herself, "I have lived in Loyang for a long time. Now I have attained the Tao, I should demonstrate the powers of the Tao to the people." Sun Pu-erh took two withered branches and blew at them softly. Instantly the two branches were transformed into a man and a woman. The woman resembled Sun Pu-erh, and the man appeared to be a handsome man in his thirties. The couple went to the busiest streets of the city and started laughing, embracing, and teasing each other. Loyang was the center of learning and culture in those days, and such shameful behaviors in public between a man and a woman in public was not tolerated. Yet despite reprimands from the city officials and the teachers of the community, the couple continued their jesting and playing day after day. Even after the guards escorted them away from the city they were found back in the busy streets the next day.

When the prominent members of the community saw that their efforts to banish the couple from the city were in vain they took counsel among themselves and approached the mayor, saying, "Many years ago, a mad woman took refuge in an abandoned house at the edge of the city. We took pity on her and gave her food when she begged. Now she is not only forgetting our kindness to her but has become a nuisance to public peace and decency. We would like to ask you to arrest this shameless couple and burn them in public. We have come to this last resort because they have ignored our pleas and our threats." One of the more powerful community leaders added, "Sir, as the leader of this city you are responsible for the good behavior of our citizens. You must do something about this shameless couple." Not wanting to offend the powerful citizens of the community, the mayor issued a decree and had it posted throughout the city. It read: "Madness is the result of losing reason. Without reason all actions become irrational. For a man and woman to embrace and tease each other in public is to break the rules of propriety. If they exhibit such shameful behavior during the day there is nothing they cannot do at night. The streets of the city are not places for jesting. To display such offensive behavior in public is abominable. We have asked them to leave, but they have refused. We have banished them from the city, but they have returned. There is only one thing left for us to do. We shall arrest them and burn them in public. Thus we can rid ourselves of these evil characters."

Together with the city guards, community leaders, and a large crowd, the mayor walked toward the abandoned house at the edge of the city where the man and the mad woman were reported to be staying. As they approached the house the mayor said, "Let everyone carry along some dry wood or twigs. We shall pile them around the house and burn the abominable place, together with the mad woman and the shameless man." The crowds piled dry branches around the building and set them on fire. Flames and smoke engulfed the building. Suddenly the grey smoke turned into a multicolored haze and the mad woman was seen seated on a canopy of clouds, flanked by the man and woman whom the people had seen jesting in the streets. Sun Pu-erh said to the crowds below, "I am a seeker of the Tao. My home is in Shantung Province, and my name is Sun Pu-erh. Twelve years ago I arrived in Loyang. I disguised myself as a mad woman so that I might pursue the path of the Tao in peace. I have finally attained the Tao, and today I shall be carried into the heavens by fire and smoke. I transformed two branches into a man and a woman so that circumstances would lead you here to witness the mystery and the powers of the Tao. In return for your kindness and hospitality to me through the years I shall give you this couple. They will be your guardians, and I shall see to it that your harvests will be plentiful and your city protected from plagues and natural disasters." Sun Pu-erh gave the man and woman a push and they fell onto the crowd below. Instantly the couple was transformed back into their original form. The crowd picked up the two branches, but when they looked up at the sky all they saw was a small black figure growing smaller and smaller as it flew higher and higher. The figure became a black dot, and

孫不二洛陽
顯道術馬丹
陽關西會友
人

子桓

Sun Pu-erh demonstrates the powers of the Tao to the residents of Loyang and ascends to heaven in a cloud of smoke.

finally the black dot disappeared. The crowds bowed their heads in respect and dispersed. For the next five years, Loyang enjoyed a prosperity that was unmatched by any town in China. Its countryside yielded bountiful harvests, and livestock was healthy and plentiful. The rains came at the appropriate times, and the city and its surrounding region seemed to be immune to natural disasters. In gratitude to Sun Pu-erh the citizens built a shrine to her. In it was a statue of her likeness, and beside her stood statues of the man and woman she had created from two branches. The shrine was named the Three Immortals' Shrine. It was said that those who presented offerings with sincerity received blessings from the three immortals.

After Sun Pu-erh ascended to the heavens she returned to the earthly realm. She wondered about the progress of Ma 'Tàn-yang and decided to offer help if needed.

When Sun Pu-erh appeared at the Ma mansion the servants could not believe that the lady of the mansion was back. They ran to tell Ma Tàn-yang, and he hurried out to greet his wife. He welcomed her home and said, "Friend in the Tào, you must have suffered much these years." Sun Pu-erh replied, "We who cultivate the Tào must bear whatever hardships beset us. Otherwise we will not be able to attain the Tào." That night, Ma Tàn-yang invited Sun Pu-erh to meditate with him. Sun Pu-erh maintained her meditation position through the night, but Ma Tàn-yang could not. The next morning Ma Tàn-yang said to Sun Pu-erh, "Friend in the Tào, your meditation skills are much more advanced than mine." Sun Pu-erh said, "Brother, I can see that your magical powers do not seem to be as strong as they could be." Ma Tàn-yang said, "You are mistaken. My magical powers are strong. I can transform stones into silver pieces. Let me show you." Sun Pu-erh said, "I can transform stones into gold, but I do not wish to do so, for gold and silver are material things that we must leave behind. Therefore it is not important whether they can be turned into silver or gold. Let me tell you a story." Then Sun Pu-erh related to Ma Tàn-yang a story about Immortals Lü Tung-pin and Chung-li Ch'üan.

When Immortal Lü Tung-pin ws studying with his teacher Chung-li Ch'üan, Chung-li Ch'üan gave him a large and heavy sack to carry. Immortal Lü carried the sack for three years without complaint or resentment. At the end of three years, Chung-li Ch'üan told Immortal Lü to open the sack. He said to Immortal Lü, "While you were carrying the sack these years, did you know what was inside?" Immortal Lü replied, "Yes, I knew that the sack was filled with stones." Chung-li Ch'üan then said, "Do you know that the rocks that you've been carrying around all these years could be turned into gold? Because you have shown sincerity and humility and have never uttered a word of complaint, I shall teach you how to turn these stones into gold if you wish." Immortal Lü asked Chung-li Ch'üan, "When these stones have been transformed into gold, will they be identical to real gold?" Chung-li Ch'üan replied, "No, gold that has been transformed from stones or other objects will only last for five hundred years. After that, they will return to their original form." Immortal Lü said, "Then I do not wish to learn the techinques of turning stones into gold. If the gold is not permanent, then what I do now will have harmful effects five hundred years later. I would rather be ignorant of a techinque which may potentially harm people." Hearing Lü Tung-pin's reply, Chung-li Chüan said, "Your foundations are stronger than mine. Your level of enlightenment will be higher than mine. As you have enlightened me, I now realize that this techinque of turning stones to gold or silver or precious gems is not worth learning and not worth teaching."

After hearing Sun Pu-erh's story, Ma Tan-yang felt ashamed and said no more. Next day, Sun Pu-erh invited Ma Tan-yang to take a bath in a tub of boiling water. Ma Tan-yang looked at the bubbling water, tested it with his finger, and exclaimed, "This water is so hot that I almost burned my finger. How can I sit in it and take a bath?" Sun Pu-erh jumped into the tub of boiling water as if it had been merely lukewarm. Turning to Ma Tan-yang, she said, "Brother, after all these years you should have cultivated a body that is impervious to heat and cold. How is it that you have not made much progress in your training?" Ma Tan-yang said, "I do not know. We received the same instructions from the same teacher. How come your meditation skill, your magical powers, and your physical development surpass mine by far?" Sun Pu-erh dried herself, put on fresh clothes and explained to Ma Tan-yang, "These twelve years I have lived in hardship. My training was done under the most adverse of conditions. Moreover, since I had to beg and live in the most meager of shelters, my body and mind were not distracted or dulled by comfortable living. You, on the other hand, lived in a comfortable house, had servants to tend your needs, and did not meet with hardships. Therefore your senses, your mind, and your body became lazy, and you did not train as hard as I did."

Ma Tan-yang said to Sun Pu-erh, "You are right. I shall leave this place and travel. I shall seek the Tao in my journeys." Late that night Ma Tan-yang changed into Taoist robes and slipped out of his mansion. The next morning Sun Pu-erh summoned the servants and told them to sell the property and distribute the money and household goods to the needy, for she knew that Ma Tan-yang would never return to his mansion and his lands again.

Ma Tang-yang left the county of Ning-hai and journeyed westward to Shensi, for he wished to visit his master's grave before he embarked on his travels. As he neared Mount Chung-nan, he saw a figure kneeling by his master's tomb. Coming closer, he recognized his brother Ch'iu Ch'ang-ch'un. He ran toward Ch'iu Ch'ang-ch'un, greeted him and said, "Brother, how have you been?" Ch'iu Ch'ang-ch'un replied, "Since the master passed away I have lingered in this area and tended his tomb. But I have not forgotten the master's teachings. All this time I have been trying to tame my heart and cultivate my original nature." Ma Tan-yang said, "Our master attained the Tao and achieved immortality. If you are still attached to the shell that he has left behind, then you have wasted the time and effort he spent in teaching you. His 'death' was a way of shedding his shell so that his spirit could be freed to ascend to the realm of immortality. Remember what our master said. Original nature is cultivated externally through virtuous acts and internally through nonattachment to forms. If you cannot relinquish your attachment to forms, then you will never tame your mind." Ch'iu Ch'ang-ch'un realized his ignorance, thanked Ma Tang-yang, and said, "Brother, if it were not for you I would have died in ignorance here." Ma Tan-yang said gently, "The master said that you would meet with more hardships than the rest of us and would require more time and training before you could attain the Tao. But be patient. Humble your intelligence and put aside your pride, and I shall impart to you what the master taught me." Ch'iu Ch'ang-ch'un thanked Ma Tang-yang again and said, "I shall remember your words, and may I prove worthy of your teachings."

Later that day Ch'iu Ch'ang-ch'un led Ma Tang-yang to the shrine built by the villagers of Ta-wei in memory of Wang Ch'ung-yang. The two disciples paid respects to their teacher and traveled for a while among the hills of Chung-nan. Ch'iu Ch'ang-ch'un kept his elder brother's words in mind and in all matters behaved humbly, not allowing his mischievous mind to play tricks and dominate his thoughts. Seeing Ch'iu Ch'ang-ch'un's sincerity and motivation to learn, Ma Tang-yang finally transmitted to him all he had learned from Wang Ch'ung-yang. Ch'iu Ch'ang-ch'un practiced diligently and progressed steadily each day.

One day Ma Tang-yang said, "Winter will be here soon. It is time we journeyed south." They gathered together what they had and followed the road south. Neither disciple had many belongings. Ch'iu Ch'ang-ch'un had what he had brought with him when he accompanied his master's bier to Shensi. Ma Tan-yang had left Ning-hai in a hurry and had not packed his meditation cushion with him. The two disciples had one meditation cushion between them and sat back to back when they mediated.

Even as they journeyed south, winter caught up with them. One night, while they rested in the ruins of a shrine, snow fell heavily. By the next morning three feet of snow had accumulated on the ground. Ch'iu Ch'ang-ch'un ventured outside, hoping to find houses nearby so that they might beg for food. But they were in an uninhabited region, a high valley surrounded by high mountains. The snow continued to fall, and the strong gusts of wind made walking difficult. The two disciples decided to wait out the storm and stayed in the abandoned shrine for three days and nights.

22

Ch'iu Ch'ang-ch'un looked at the snow-covered ground and thought to himself, "My brother came from a rich family. He is not used to hardships such as hunger and cold. I should go out and see if I can find something hot for him to eat." So, while Ma Tan-yang was meditating, Ch'iu Ch'ang-ch'un slipped out of the shrine. Snowdrifts four to five feet high were piled everywhere. The path they had followed was hidden. Not only could Ch'iu Ch'ang-ch'un make no progress through the trails, but here and there snow roared down the slopes in avalanches. Sadly, Ch'iu Ch'ang-ch'un walked back into the abandoned shrine. There was nothing to do but wait for the snow to melt.

Ch'iu Ch'ang-ch'un decided to pass his time in meditation. He sat down on the cushion with his back to Ma Tan-yang but no matter how hard he tried to stop his thoughts, he could not banish the thoughts of getting food for Ma Tan-yang from his mind. His thoughts were so strong that they reached the ears of the earth god of the shrine. Seeing the plight of the two Taoist monks, the earth god hurriedly visited a kindly old man who lived in a hut tucked away in a nearby valley. Presenting himself to the old man in a dream, the earth god said, "In my shrine are two Taoist monks who have been without food and water for the last three days. Get up quickly and prepare a hot meal for them." The old man woke up, roused his wife, and related his dream to her. The pious woman believed strongly in gods and spirits and immediately went into the kitchen to prepare two full bowls of rice and vegetables. The commotion in the house woke up her son and her daughter-in-law. When they were informed of their father's dream they said, "Mother, we would be glad to carry the food to the shrine." The couple found the shrine and presented the food to Ma Tan-yang and Ch'iu Ch'ang-ch'un. Ma Tan-yang thought that the couple were local residents who had known that they were trapped in the shrine. He thanked the couple for their kindness and ate the rice and food they brought. Ma Tan-yang was about to return to his meditation cushion when Ch'iu Ch'ang-ch'un said, "Brother, the ways of the Tao are mysterious. Last night I thought about getting food for you while I was trying to meditate and today someone brought us food." Ma Tan-yang looked at Ch'iu Ch'ang-ch'un and said angrily, "Those who seek the Tao forget their hunger. All you can think of is food! When are you ever going to learn? I have had enough of you! Today we shall part and never meet again." With a quick stroke of his knife, Ma Tan-yang cut the meditation cushion in two. He took one half of it and handed the other half to Ch'iu Ch'ang-ch'un saying, "Brother, work hard and discipline yourself so that your future will not be ruined." Then he walked swiftly out of the shrine.

Ch'iu Ch'ang-ch'un hurried after him, but Ma Tan-yang had disappeared. He ran down the slope of the mountain calling for his elder brother, but there was no answer. Evening came, and Ch'iu Ch'ang-ch'un saw a figure in the distance. Thinking it was Ma Tan-yang, he ran toward the figure but found that it was a woodcutter returning home with his load of firewood. When Ch'iu Ch'ang-ch'un asked the woodcutter if he had seen a Taoist monk in the area, the woodcutter replied, "Master, I have been cutting wood in this area all day but have seen no one." He then added, "Sir, it is getting dark, and the wild animals will be out soon. Come to my hut and spend the night. Tomorrow morning you can continue to look for you friend." Ch'iu Ch'ang-ch'un thanked him and said, "I must be on my way. If I tarry here for the night, I shall never find him. But, kind sir, if you could climb up a tree and call loudly for my friend to wait for me, I would be grateful to you for the rest of my life." The woodcutter climbed up a tall tree and shouted, "Taoist master, please stay and wait, please stay and wait." His voice echoed in the mountains but there was no response.

As soon as Ma Tan-yang left the shrine he used his magical powers to travel underground. Within a short time he had left the mountains of southwest China and arrived at the Kao mountains in Honan Province in central China. There he attained the Tao and left the earthly realm.

Ch'iu Ch'ang-ch'un knew that with Ma Tan-yang's departure

大圜蒲分
道情戀不
當法相問
量人把面

*Ch'iu Ch'ang-ch'un meets with a diviner and is told that he
will die of hunger.*

129

he was the only one of the seven disciples of Wang Ch'ung-yang left. He no longer could rely on the others to help him. Remembering Ma Tan-yang's words, he decided to cultivate emptiness in his thinking, feeling, and sensing. To remind himself of his goal, he composed a poem:

> Let my mind forget about eating and drinking.
> If I think of comfort and riches, let my bones and
>   tendons wither.
> If I think of food and water, let my mouth be plagued
>   with boils.
> Let my body be an empty vessel where nothing can be
>   stored.

He wrote the poem on a piece of wood and placed it before him. Every day he meditated in front of these words.

One day as he passed by a small town he saw a large mansion off the main road. He walked up to the door, knocked on it, and called out to the residents that a monk was standing outside begging for food. The door opened and a young servant handed him a bowl of rice and vegetables. Ch'iu Ch'ang-ch'un sat down on the doorstep and was about to eat when an elderly man came out and took the bowl from Ch'iu Ch'ang-ch'un. Ch'iu Ch'ang-ch'un bowed to the man and said, "Sir, if I have offended you, please let me know so that I can apologize. And if I have not offended you, why did you take the food away from me? Is it because I am not worthy of receiving your kindness, or is it that you do not like our kind?" The old man laughed and said, "Monk, it is not I who do not wish to help. It is you who are destined not to receive it." Ch'iu Ch'ang-ch'un said, "Sir, please explain. Why am I not destined to receive food from you?" The old man replied, "I have studied divination since I was a child. I can tell from your looks that you are destined to die of hunger. Moreover, every morsel you eat will bring you more hardship. If it is the will of heaven, why not comply?" Ch'iu Ch'ang-ch'un said, "Sir, since you are a man who can foretell the future, can you tell me if I will attain the Tao in this lifetime?" The old man scrutinized Ch'iu Ch'ang-ch'un closely, shook his head, and said, "On your face it is written that you will not be able to accomplish your task as long as you live." Ch'iu Ch'ang-ch'un said, "Sir, is there no other outcome?" The man said, "What is written by destiny must happen, however incredible it may sound when it is foretold. Let me give you some examples, and perhaps you will understand.

"In the time of the Warring States [475–221 B.C.E.], the ruler of the kingdom of Chu was told that he would die of hunger. He laughed and said that it would be impossible for a king to die of hunger. Some years later, his two sons fought each other for the right to be their father's heir. The old king was held captive in the palace by the princes, who were afraid that their father might favor one or the other. The quarrel over the succession involved everyone in the palace. Even the servants and the cooks were drafted into fighting for one prince or the other. The old king was locked in his chamber and was deprived of food for seven days. On the eighth day, the king discovered that a bird had laid several eggs in a nest that perched on the ceiling beams. He climbed up to the beams and was about to reach for the eggs when the mother bird returned to her nest. The bird defended her nest furiously. Fumbling about, the king knocked the nest over the beam. The eggs fell to the floor, and before the king could get to them they were eaten by a rat. One the ninth day the old king died of hunger.

"There is another story about a nobleman by the name of T'ang who lived in the Han dynasty [206 B.C.E.–219 C.E.]. One day, Lord T'ang met a fortune-teller who told him that he would die of hunger. T'ang was a superstitious man, and the fortune-teller's words bothered him. He went to the emperor and said, "Sire, a fortune-teller told me that I would die of hunger. All my life I have served the country. I have never taken more than was allotted to me. I have given freely to the poor, and as a result I have never been able to accumulate wealth. I am afraid that after I retire from government service my family and I will starve to death." The emperor said to him, "You are an educated man. Why do you believe the words of a fortune-teller? Still, whether you believe him or not you do not need to worry. You have served me well, and I shall reward you. I shall give you a piece of land on which a rich iron mine is located. You and your descendants will never lack wealth and prosperity."

"Within ten years Lord T'ang's yearly income grew from one thousand gold pieces to one million gold pieces. He became the talk of the capital and the envy of the nobility. You may ask, how could such a rich man starve to death? However, twelve years later the emperor died of an incurable illness, and his son ascended the throne. Many nobles thought that this would be their opportunity to cut down Lord T'ang's power and wealth. They approached the young emperor and told him that Lord T'ang was using his wealth to buy weapons and train a large army, and that he was plotting to claim the throne for himself. Swayed by his court advisors, the emperor ordered Lord T'ang arrested and thrown into prison. His adversaries bribed the prison guards, and T'ang was not given food or water for seven days. On the eight day, one kindly jailer who did not have the heart to starve the old man to death handed him a bowl of soup. But before Lord T'ang could swallow the soup, the captain of the guards knocked the bowl out of his hand. Thus Lord T'ang starved to death in prison. Then there is the story of two hermits, Po I and Shu Ch'i, who knew that it was their destiny to die of starvation. The two men refused knighthood by the emperor and starved themselves to death in the mountains. Thus, if destiny prescribes that one is to die of hunger, there is no escape."

After hearing the old man's stories, Ch'iu Ch'ang-ch'un left the mansion deep in thought. He decided to follow the destiny of heaven and the example of the two hermits who lived their short lives in accordance with what had been planned for them by the gods. He walked west toward the mountains where Po I and Shu Ch'i had starved themselves to death. There he saw a deep gorge carved by a swift river. Boulders lined the river bank, and huge outcrops of rock protruded from the river bed, barring the path of the angry white waters. Ch'iu Ch'ang-ch'un climbed down the gorge into the depths of the canyon. For nine days and nights he sat on a boulder by the river, waiting to die of hunger and thirst. Most people would have died under such circumstances, but Ch'iu Ch'ang-ch'un was one with a strong foundation in Taoist training. Nine days without food and water did not weaken him, and the fasting merely cleared his mind and sharpened his senses. On the tenth day, a rainstorm along the upper course of the river produced a flash flood in the canyon. The river rose several feet and roared down the gorge with tremendous force. The waters rushed to where Ch'iu Ch'ang-ch'un was sitting, but Ch'iu Ch'ang-ch'un did not budge. He was determined to perish in the flood if he did not die of hunger. As he watched the waters close in he saw a branch floating toward him. As the branch rested in front of him he saw a large red peach attached to the branch. "This is strange," he said to himself. "This branch seemed to come from nowhere, yet it was borne on the waves of these angry waters to rest in front of me. I wonder if it was meant for me to eat." He took a bite, and the peach was so delicious that he swallowed the fruit in one mouthful. Suddenly his body was filled with energy. At the same time, the flood waters receded and the sun shone brightly. Ch'iu Ch'ang-ch'un took this to be an omen from the gods that he was not meant to die by the river. He got up and headed for the trail that would lead him out of the canyon.

23

Ch'iu Ch'ang=ch'un left the river gorge and walked east toward the mountains known as T'ai Shan. He climbed up the trail and found a mountain shrine tucked away in the desolate peaks. There he lay down beside the altar and closed his eyes. For nine days and nights he did not touch food or water. On the tenth day, he heard voices outside the shrine. The din of voices became louder, and soon footsteps could be heard. As Ch'iu Ch'ang-ch'un turned toward the door he saw a burly fellow entering the courtyard of the shrine, saying, "I'll clean up this place a bit so that we can cook our supper here." The fellow looked at Ch'iu Ch'ang-ch'un and obviously did not know what to make of a starving monk in a remote shrine; then he walked outside to gather firewood. Meanwhile, other voices were heard in the courtyard and more men arrived, bringing cooking utensils and wild game. The men settled in the courtyard and starting cooking. The smell of the food reached Ch'iu Ch'ang-ch'un, but he kept his vigil by the altar. He could hear the men talking and joking over their supper. One man said, "Brothers, let us drink and celebrate. We have not hauled in this much loot in a long time. I think each one is going to be satisfied with his share." The man who was speaking was named Chao Pi; he was the leader of the group. Chao Pi and his "brothers" were a gang of robbers who occasionally used the mountain shrine as a hideout. That day they had managed to rob a merchant caravan, and now they were planning to divide the loot after celebrating their success. Chao Pi and his friends had become robbers after having been turned out of their homes by corrupt officials in a series of unfair legal settlements. Initially they had been driven to robbery because they had no money with which to set up an honest business. However, they had now become accustomed to living outside the law and were no longer eager to return to a more honest livelihood.

After several rounds of toasts, one of the men, the burly fellow who had seen Ch'iu Ch'ang-ch'un, said to Chao Pi, "Brother, we have done many things against the will of Heaven. I do not doubt that we will be punished after we die. Let us perform a good deed so that our punishment will be lessened. There is a starving Taoist monk in the shrine who is about to die. Let us give him some of our food and save his life, for it is said that helping a holy man is a good deed that Heaven will not forget." Chao Pi said, "That is a very good idea. Let us feed this monk. Maybe he can pray to the gods for us and lessen our karmic retribution."

Chao Pi and his men walked over to where Ch'iu Ch'ang-ch'un lay and offered him a bowl of rice and noodles, but Ch'iu Ch'ang-ch'un refused to eat. Seeing that the monk was determined not to eat, Chao Pi took the food and forced it down Ch'iu Ch'ang-ch'un's mouth. Ch'iu Ch'ang-ch'un swallowed involuntarily; then he spat out the rest of the food and said, "Why are you tormenting me? Every morsel I swallow will increase my misery. If you want to help me, then leave me alone." One of the robbers said, "You ungrateful monk! We are trying to help you, and you will not accept our kindness. Well, if you want to be stubborn, we'll kill you and satisfy your wish to die." He pulled out a knife and pointed it at Ch'iu Ch'ang-ch'un's throat. Ch'iu Ch'ang-ch'un said, "If you wish to kill me, then thrust your knife into my belly. You forced me to accept food that I did not want. Now you can open up my stomach and take it back." The robber was about to stab Ch'iu Ch'ang-ch'un when Chao Pi reached out and wrenched the knife from the man's hand. Turning to his men, he said, "Brothers, we should not kill this monk. He is a brave man, and do you not know that the karma you would reap from killing a holy man would haunt your family for generations?" He then said to Ch'iu Ch'ang-ch'un, "Taoist master, it appears that you are determined to die. Can you at least tell us why you wish death?" Ch'iu Ch'ang-ch'un replied, "I met a fortune-teller who told me that I was destined to die of hunger and that what is written by destiny should not be opposed by the action of man. Therefore, like the sages Po I and Shu Ch'i, I am determined to starve myself to death." Chao Pi said, "Master, do you really believe in the empty sayings of fortune-tellers? Abandon your quest for death. Find some remote shrine. Get yourself a disciple. We can give you some money so that you

化強梁改邪迴正
談至理因死得生

Ch'iu Ch'ang-ch'un meets robbers outside a mountain shrine
in T'ai Shan.

can live in a shrine and meditate to your heart's content." Chao Pi took some silver coins and placed them in a small sack, which he handed to Ch'iu Ch'ang-ch'un. But Ch'iu Ch'ang-ch'un shook his head and said, "I appreciate your kindness, but I have made an oath that I will not accept other people's money or possessions." He brought forth the small wooden plaque and showed it to the bandits. Years ago when he had parted with Ma Tan-yang he had made the plaque and had inscribed it with words to remind him of the goal of his training: to be empty of desire and thoughts. The robbers looked at the writing and said, "We are giving you money out of our own free will. It has nothing to do with your wanting what we have. Why will you not take our gift?" Ch'iu Ch'ang-ch'un replied, "I do not deserve your gift, because in my past life I did not give freely to those in need. Therefore in this lifetime I need to repay those to whom I owe debts from my previous lifetimes. If I receive anything from you it will only add to my karmic retribution. The law of karma says that what you do must be repaid. If you take something away from someone, you have to give it back. If you help someone you will be repaid in full." Hearing this, Chao Pi said, "Sir, if this is so, then all of us will reap severe karmic retribution in our future lives since we have stolen and robbed in this life." Ch'iu Ch'ang-ch'un said, "You are robbers now because in your previous lives you were robbed and treated unfairly. Those who treated you unjustly in their previous lives are paying for it now. However, if you continue to rob others after they have fully paid for their evil deeds, then you will reap karmic retribution for yourselves and your families." Hearing this, Chao Pi said, "We have been paid back in full for what was owed us in our previous lives. If we continue to rob we will have to pay for our deeds in our future lives. It is time we stopped." Turning to Ch'iu Ch'ang-ch'un, he said, "Master, we thank you for your advice. If we had not met you we would have accumulated heavy retribution on ourselves and our families." He then stood up and said in an authoritative voice, "Brothers, we should stop being robbers. In the years since we have lived outside the law we have managed to accumulate some riches. Let us put our money into business investments and lead a lawful life from now on." The men nodded in agreement. As the robbers prepared to leave, Chao Pi bid farewell to Ch'iu Ch'ang-ch'un and said, "Master, I shall be grateful to you for the rest of my life. Perhaps in another lifetime we will meet again and I shall become your disciple."

Ch'iu Ch'ang-ch'un walked down the slopes alone dejectedly. Twice he had wanted to die of starvation, but twice he had been prevented from doing so. Over the next few months Ch'iu Ch'ang-ch'un begged for small coins in the nearby towns. Then he brought an iron chain. He carried the chain into a heavily forested region of Tai Shan and found a spot where the trees were tall and their branches thick. He climbed up a tree and fastened one end of the chain around a thick branch and the other end around his neck. "This time I shall surely die, for there is no one here to stop me." But while Ch'iu Ch'ang-ch'un was planning to hang himself, the Lord of the star T'ai-pai was alerted by the earth-god. The heavenly lord immediately assumed the form of an herb gatherer and appeared under the tree where Ch'iu Ch'ang-ch'un was about to hang himself. Ch'iu Ch'ang-ch'un was so busy fastening the chain around the branch and his neck that he did not see the figure standing below him. The herb gatherer called out to Ch'iu Ch'ang-ch'un, "Why are you trying to end your life? What have you done to deserve this ending?" Annoyed, Ch'iu Ch'ang-ch'un looked down and said, "What I do is none of your business." The herb gatherer said, "I am a follower of the Tao, and the life and death of sentient beings is my business. The Tao values the life of all things. Why don't you tell me why you wish to take your own life?" Ch'iu Ch'ang-ch'un said, "All right, I'll tell why I need to die. Some time ago I met a fortune-teller who told me that I was destined to die of hunger and that I should never attain enlightenment in this lifetime. My two attempts at starvation have failed. That is why I came here to hang myself. I wish to end my life now before anybody else interferes." The herb gatherer said, "So you wanted to die after listening to one man's words. Maybe another man's words will bring you back to your senses. Your mind is invaded by monsters, and your wisdom is clouded. Your folly has not only almost taken your life but also ruined your chances of becoming an immortal in this lifetime. Listen to what I have to say, and the monsters who have captured your mind will leave you." The herb gatherer sat down, motioned Ch'iu Ch'ang-ch'un to sit beside him, and said, "The lines of destiny written on your face are not true indicators of your destiny. For the true face is not your physical face but the face of your mind. And it is on the face of your mind that true destiny is written. Therefore, when the fortune-tellers say that a person has a kind disposition or a cruel disposition written on his or her face, they are merely referring to a minor determinant of destiny. The major determinant of destiny is in the heart. If a cruel heart is tamed, or a kind heart becomes cruel, the external features will change. Therefore, the facial appearance is merely an indicator of the destiny written on the internal face, which is your heart. Our destiny is determined by our own actions. People who were initially destined to die peacefully may end their lives in violence if they do evil deeds. People who were initially destined to die a violent death may die peacefully if they perform good deeds. Our destiny is in our own hands. Those who could not escape death by starvation were people who had hoarded grain, pillaged storage houses, or refused to alleviate famine. Retribution was inescapable. But as for you, you are supposed to be trained in the path of the Tao and yet you fell into the clutches of external forms and let your attachment to appearance ruin you. As a Taoist adept, you should know that immortality is within the reach of everyone and that it is up to our own efforts to make it a reality. You should know that it is not the 'destiny' written on your face that determines whether you will achieve enlightenment but the effort that you make."

The herb gatherer's words hit Ch'iu Ch'ang-ch'un like cold water. He felt as if he had been jolted out of a bad dream. Everything now made sense. He thought to himself, "How stupid of me! How could I have been so blind! From now on I shall throw off my preoccupation with death. I shall complete my training and attain the Tao."

24

The herb gatherer helped Ch'iu Ch'ang-ch'un unfasten the chain from around his neck. Ch'iu Ch'ang-ch'un thanked him and said, "Sir, if not for you, I would still be held captive by the monsters of my mind. I shall never forget what you have done for me." The herb gatherer said, "You need not thank me. I did not give you money or food. I only uttered a few words. It was up to you to believe them or not. You liberated yourself from the monsters of the mind by realizing that it was your folly that trapped you into your preoccupation with death." After saying these words, the herb gatherer disappeared.

Ch'iu Ch'ang-ch'un looked around him and saw everything in a new light. The forest was dancing in the sunlight, and the air was pure and fragrant. It was as if a fog had lifted and an unlimted view was now laid out before him. From that moment Ch'iu Ch'ang-ch'un abandoned his morbid thoughts and began his training again with renewed strength and vigor. As Ch'iu Ch'ang-ch'un's experiences show, the monsters of the mind play dangerous tricks with our thoughts. If the root of evil is not severed, then even a heavenly army cannot defeat these monsters. No matter where one runs, the monsters will follow. But fortunately for Ch'iu Ch'ang-ch'un, the Lord of the star T'ai-pai helped him rid himself of the root of evil, and Ch'iu Ch'ang-ch'un was able to free himself from the illusions that evil was capable of weaving.

Ch'iu Ch'ang-ch'un now left the forests of T'ai Shan and wandered south. One day in the midst of a hot summer he reached a river whose bank was strewn with small stones. The river was wide and calm, but it was difficult to tell from its appearance how deep the waters were. Ch'iu Ch'ang-ch'un walked along its banks for a long time and was puzzled that there were no bridges or ferries. As he was wondering how he was going to cross the river, he saw some men approaching. Ch'iu Ch'ang-ch'un walked up to them and asked respectfully, "Sirs, I am trying to cross the river. Can you tell me where I can find a bridge or a ferry?" The men laughed good-naturedly and said,

"Taoist master, you must be foreign to this area. The river is very shallow in some places. You could easily wade across. We've never had a need for bridges or ferries. Come, we'll show you where the shallow waters are." Just as the men had told him, there was a section of the river that was only waist-deep. Ch'iu Ch'ang-ch'un walked across and sat down on the rocks. Suddenly he had an idea. "If the shallow waters are known only to the local people, then it must be a trial for those who are foreign to this area to find a way to cross the river. Besides, it would be difficult for the elderly and the weak to cross the river by wading. I can make myself useful to others by carrying them across."

Thus Ch'iu Ch'ang-ch'un built a small shack by the ford of the river. Daily he carried people across. He made his living by begging in the nearby villages and by the small amount of coins that grateful travelers gave him for carrying them across. But Ch'iu Ch'ang-ch'un never asked for payment. He accepted what was given him. Even if he received nothing in return he would still do his work cheerfully. During the six years that Ch'iu Ch'ang-ch'un carried people across the river, neither wind, nor rain, nor storm could stop him. His fame spread, and many people came to regard him as an immortal. One day, as he was meditating, his spirit was freed and journeyed long distances before returning. He now understood Wang Ch'ung-yang's words "Your hardships will not end until you have reach the river that runs over many stones." Beside a river that deposited many stones along its banks, Ch'iu Ch'ang-ch'un attained enlightenment.

One day it was exceptionally stormy. The wind whipped the river into a wild roaring foam. Ch'iu Ch'ang-ch'un looked out of the window of his shack and said, "Nobody would travel on a day like this." Scarcely had he finished his remark when he heard a knock. He opened the door and saw three men dressed like police captains. One of the men said to Ch'iu Ch'ang-ch'un, "We would like you to take us across the river. We are on a mission, and we need to reach the magistrate's court tomorrow." The second man added, "We have killed the most notorious bandit in the area and are carrying his head to be displayed in the court." The third man held up a bloody bundle to show Ch'iu Ch'ang-

苦根盡相隨
心變
陰魔起幻由
人生

Ch'iu Ch'ang-ch'un carries the three captains across the river.
Ch'iu Ch'ang-ch'un is visited by the monsters of attachment.

ch'un. Ch'iu Ch'ang-ch'un said, "Very well, I shall carry you across."

As they approached the ford, the river had already risen several feet and was no longer waist-deep. When Ch'iu Ch'ang-ch'un stepped into the river, the water was up to his neck. He walked through the raging waters in steady strides and carried the first and second captains across. As the third captain had climbed onto his back and Ch'iu Ch'ang-ch'un was about to step into the river, the captain said, "I suffer from water phobia, and I am terribly afraid of drowning. Please walk carefully." Ch'iu Ch'ang-ch'un said, "Do not worry. Wrap your arms around my neck and hold on tight." As he walked, Ch'iu Ch'ang-ch'un could feel the man on his back shaking in fear. Halfway across the river, the captain slipped from Ch'iu Ch'ang-ch'un's back and fell into the river. Ch'iu Ch'ang-ch'un quickly hauled him out of the water, hoisted him onto his back, and said, "Try to relax and you will not be afraid." But the man said, "My life may have been saved for the time being, but the bundle with the bandit's head was swept away when I fell. If I do not present evidence to the magistrate that the bandit has been killed, I shall be beheaded." Ch'iu Ch'ang-ch'un set the captain down on the other side of the river and said, "A head is what you need to save you from being punished. Here, cut off my head. Smear it with blood and take it to the magistrate." The captain said, "Thank you for your kindness. But I will not kill an innocent man, let alone one who has just saved my life." Ch'iu Ch'ang-ch'un said, "If you cannot cut off my head, then I shall do it for you." He took the captain's sword from its sheath and was about to slash his neck when a voice from Heaven boomed, "Ch'iu Ch'ang-ch'un, do not kill yourself. Give the sword back to us." Ch'iu Ch'ang-ch'un looked up and saw a rainbow-colored cloud. On it stood the three captains whom he had carried across the river. They said to him, "Ch'iu Ch'ang-ch'un, we are the Lords of the Three Seasons and Keepers of the Heavenly, Earth, and Water Realms. Your personal sacrifice has moved the Lords of Heaven. They will replace your mortal body with an immortal body and your mortal spirit with an immortal spirit. In seven years you will ascend to the palace of the Empress of Heaven." Ch'iu Ch'ang-ch'un took a step and found that he was immediately transported to the palace of the Heavenly Lords. He bowed to the Lords of the Three Seasons and returned the sword to them.

When Ch'iu Ch'ang-ch'un returned to the earthly realm he thought to himself, "Now that I have finally attained an immortal body, I'd like to visit that fortune-teller again and see what he has to say. A few years ago he was confident that I was to die of starvation." So Ch'iu Ch'ang-ch'un journeyed to the village where he had met the fortune-teller. He knocked on the door and a young man appeared. This young man was none other than the servant boy who had given him food when he had begged at this same door years ago. The young man was astonished to see Ch'iu Ch'ang-ch'un and greeted him, saying, "I am so glad you are still alive." Ch'iu Ch'ang-ch'un said, "Could you please lead me to your master? There are a few things that I would like to clarify with him." When Ch'iu Ch'ang-ch'un saw the fortune-teller, he said, "Sir, do you remember me?" The fortune-teller replied, "My memory escapes me. You look familiar, but I do not remember who you are." Ch'iu Ch'ang-ch'un said, "Sir, a few years ago I passed by this village and begged for food at your door. You looked at my face and said that I was destined to die of starvation." The fortune-teller said, "Oh yes, you are that Taoist monk." Ch'iu Ch'ang-ch'un said, "Sir, you were wrong in your divination. I not only did not die, but have attained enlightenment." The fortune-teller laughed and said, "Taoist master, I was not mistaken back then. A few years ago, your face had the characteristics that mark you as a man who would die of hunger, but now those features are gone from your face. As a matter of fact, your face now tells me that you are destined to become an immortal and that you will be given a large monastery by the emperor and your disciples will carry your teachings to the ends of the world." Ch'iu Ch'ang-ch'un was suddenly ashamed. He had come with the malicious intent of exposing the fortune-teller's mistake. Now he understood what the herb gatherer had meant when he said that the heart determines the facial features, and that if the heart changes, then the facial characteristics will change. Destiny and karma are not determined by Heaven but are built from human actions.

Ch'iu Ch'ang-ch'un left the fortune-teller's mansion and took shelter that night in an abandoned shrine. While he was meditating, a strong gust of wind blew in from the window and a shroud of fog enveloped him. Because he had harbored a trace of malicious intent toward the fortune-teller, the monsters of the mind returned to plague him. A ferocious tiger appeared in front of Ch'iu Ch'ang-ch'un and snarled. Remembering Wang Ch'ung-yang's teachings, he continued meditating as if nothing had happened. The tiger disappeared, and a young Taoist apprentice stood at the door of the shrine saying, "My master Ma Tan-yang is on his way here. Won't you get up and meet him outside?" The boy disappeared and Ch'iu Ch'ang-ch'un saw the familiar figure of Ma Tan-yang walking along a mountain trail. Ch'iu Ch'ang-ch'un said aloud, "In the Tao there are no attachments. If he comes, then let him come. If he leaves, then let him leave." The image of Ma Tan-yang disappeared, and in his place was a large crowd of people, men and women, young and old. They said to him, "Taoist master, you carried us across the river through sun and rain. We have gathered together one bushel of rice and a sack of gold. Come get your reward, and you will have enough to see you through this lifetime."

Ch'iu Ch'ang-ch'un ignored them and continued meditating. The image of the crowd dissolved and a young girl stood in front him. She was dressed in rags and her arms and legs were covered with bruises. Ch'iu Ch'ang-ch'un heard her say, "Kind sir, please escort me to my uncle's home. My stepmother has beaten me and turned me out of the house. If you help me, my uncle shall reward you well." Ch'iu Ch'ang-ch'un acted as if nothing had happened. The image of the girl disappeared and his sister-in-law appeared saying, "Your elder brother died of an unknown illness, and your uncle has taken over your father's property. He has given us three days' notice to leave. My children and I have nowhere to go. Come back quickly and put things right." At the same time, Ch'iu Ch'ang-ch'un's nephews and nieces appeared, tugging at his sleeves saying, "Uncle, please come home. Our father is dead. We will all be beggars if you won't help us." Ch'iu Ch'ang-ch'un continued meditating. The images of the children and his sister-in-law disappeared. Soon after that the fog lifted.

Only the occasinal rustle of dry leaves could be heard. In the stillness of the night, Ch'iu Ch'ang-ch'un suddenly heard a crack of thunder. He looked up to the sky and saw the gates of Heaven open. Two children appeared, mounted on the back of a stork. The stork flew to where Ch'iu Ch'ang-ch'un was sitting and the children invited him to ascend to the gates of Heaven with them.

25

Ch'iu Ch'ang=ch'un thought to himself, "The Lords of Heaven, Earth, and Water told me that I need to cultivate myself for seven more years before I can attain immortality. The stork and the immortal children must be illusions. The monsters of my mind are playing tricks on me again." The vision suddenly dissolved, and Ch'iu Ch'ang-ch'un found himself sitting alone in the abandoned shrine. He looked outside and saw the moon and the stars against a dark sky. Ch'iu Ch'ang-ch'un said to himself, "Because I harbored an intention to challenge the fortune-teller, my mind is being constantly attacked by illusions. If I do not find a way to dissolve these monsters, the *yin* energies will remain in my body and I shall never attain a body of purity."

Ch'iu Ch'ang-ch'un thought for a long time and finally came upon a plan. He found a small hill and built a grass hut at the bottom of the slope. Next to his hut he placed a large boulder. Whenever false visions appeared, he would push the boulder up the hill and roll it down the slope. Then he would return to his hut to meditate. For three years Ch'iu Ch'ang-ch'un meditated and pushed the boulder up the hill when his mind was invaded by illusions. Finally, he dissolved the last trace of ego from his mind.

One night as Ch'iu Ch'ang-ch'un was meditating, he felt that he was being commanded to go to a village to warn a person of impending disaster. He followed his intuition and arrived at a village that hugged the banks of a river. In this village was a wealthy man by the name of Wang Yün. Wang Yün owned most of the land surrounding the village and collected rents from the peasants who leased his land for farming. Wang Yün was the richest man in the village, but he was miserly and cruel. If his tenants did not pay their rent on time he would force them to sell their livestock and grain. He loaned money at high interest rates, and many villagers were forced to sell their children when they could not repay on time. Knowing that their master controlled the livelihood of the village, Wang Yün's servants bullied the farmers and merchants. They looted stores and barns. They raped young girls. They robbed defenseless old men and women.

Wang Yün's mansion was built close to the river bank. The river and the willows on its bank provided a scenic setting for the gazebos and miniature mountains that formed the front garden of the Wang mansion. Away from the river on the edge of the Wang estate was a hill. One of Wang Yün's ancestors had built a shrine for Kuan-yin. In previous generations the shrine had been visited frequently by members of the Wang family, but in Wang Yün time the shrine was abandoned, for Wang Yün despised the ways of Buddhism and Taoism. When Ch'iu Ch'ang-ch'un arrived in the village he settled in the abandoned shrine. Each day he went to the Wang mansion to beg for meals. Each day he was turned away by Wang Yün's servants. On the twelfth day, when Ch'iu Ch'ang-ch'un knocked at the door, a young servant girl by the name of Ch'un-Hua appeared. She glanced around to make sure that no one was looking before she gave Ch'iu Ch'ang-ch'un some steamed buns. Softly she said, "Taoist master, accept this food and please go away before my master finds out that you are here." Then she slipped quietly back into the mansion.

For the next two days Ch'un-Hua brought Ch'iu Ch'ang-ch'un rice and noodles and steamed rolls. On the third day, as Ch'iu Ch'ang-ch'un was about to knock on the door, Wang Yün appeared with his entourage of servants. When Ch'iu Ch'ang-ch'un saw Wang Yün he said, "Craving fame and fortune will ruin your life. If you are able to detach yourself from material goods then your mind will be free of anxiety. You cannot take gold and silver with you when you die. You leave with only the trace of tears from your eyes." Ch'iu Ch'ang-ch'un had intended to warn Wang Yün that if he continued his evil ways disaster would be imminent. But instead of realizing his wrongs, Wang Yün looked at Ch'iu Ch'ang-ch'un and said angrily, "You scoundrel of a monk, what are you talking about? I want no dealings with Buddhists and Taoists. You had better go before I set the dogs on you." Ch'iu Ch'ang-ch'un replied calmly, "Sir, I was passing by your village and all I am asking for is a meal." Wang Yün laughed and joked with his servants, "Hey, this monk wants a meal. Let's give him one." Wang Yün whispered to a servant, and the latter

真陽足
葷陰退
散惡貫
盈合家
沉淪

Ch'iu Ch'ang-ch'un is given horse dung when he begs at the house of Wang Yün.

took a shovel, walked to the stables, and returned with a pile of horse dung. Wang Yün took the shovel, thrust it at Ch'iu Ch'ang-ch'un, and said, "Here, have your dinner." Ch'iu Ch'ang-ch'un said, "Do not jest with a poor old monk." Wang Yün and his servants laughed and went inside the mansion.

All this time Ch'un-Hua had been standing behind a pillar. She could not bear the cruel behavior of her master and her fellow servants. After her master was gone she approached Ch'iu Ch'ang-ch'un and said, "Taoist master, here are some rice cakes. Take them or you'll be hungry tonight." Ch'iu Ch'ang-ch'un said, "Today I did not come to beg for food. I came to warn your master that if he did not repent his evil deeds, disaster would come to his household. Since he did not listen, karma will see to it that he does not escape what will befall him. Because you do not participate in the cruel deeds of the members of this household, my word of warning is now given to you instead." Ch'iu Ch'ang-ch'un then took Ch'un-Hua behind a group of trees and whispered to her, "If you see the eyes of the stone lions in front of the mansion turn red, then you must hurry to the shrine of Kuan-yin and stay there on the hill for about two hours. Whatever happens, do not return to your master's mansion during that time." Ch'iu Ch'ang-ch'un then disappeared.

Ch'un-Hua returned to her master's mansion. Outwardly she acted as if nothing had happened, but in her mind she remembered the words of Ch'iu Ch'ang-ch'un. Every morning she slipped out of the front door of the mansion and examined the eyes of the two stone lions that guarded the entrance. This went on for two months. One day, as she was coming out to check the lions' eyes a cowherd stopped her and said, "Lady, every morning when I take the cows out to the field I see you looking intently at these stone lions. You have been doing this for the past two months. Can you tell me what is so interesting about these lions?" Ch'un-Hua said, "Little brother, a while ago a Taoist monk came to beg for food at my master's mansion and told me that if the lions' eyes turned red I should run to the shrine of Kuan-yin and stay there for two hours. That is why I am checking the lions' eyes every morning."

When the cowherd heard Ch'un-Hua's words he said to himself, "Let me play a trick on her." So late that night he took some red dye and smeared it on the stone lions' eyes. Quietly he hid behind a tree to wait for Ch'un-Hua to appear in the morning. But that night while Ch'un-Hua was about to fall asleep, her heart started beating wildly. She sat up, and sweat poured down her brow. Suddenly the thought came to her mind, "Go check the eyes of the lions!" She leapt out of bed and ran out the front door. When she saw that the eyes of the lions were indeed red, she hurried toward the shrine of Kuan-yin on the hill. The cowherd, wanting to know what happened, ran after her. As the two reached the shrine, a loud clap of thunder resounded. Rain poured down, and the earth shook. Ch'un-Hua and the cowherd crawled under the altar table and held on to each other. In the distance they could hear buildings collapse and trees crashing to the ground. They did not dare to come out of the shrine until sunlight appeared the next morning. Stunned, they walked back to the village. As they approached, they saw that the mansion of Wang Yün had disappeared from the face of the earth. Here and there were uprooted trees, but no sign of life was seen. A crowd of villagers gathered at the site where the Wang mansion had stood. One old man said, "The Lords of Heaven must have commanded the river gods to sweep the accursed mansion away. Karma has finally caught up with Master Wang and his arrogant servants." Ch'un-Hua's sobs brought the villagers' attention to her. One elderly farmer said to her, "Ch'un-Hua, your master and his servants all disappeared in the flood caused by the earthquake. How is it that your survived?" When Ch'un-Hua explained to the villagers that she had been warned by a Taoist monk, people nodded and said, "The Taoist monk must be an immortal sent by the Lords of Heaven. Those who are kindhearted will be warned of impending disasters." A woman said to Ch'un-Hua, "You are now homeless. What will you do?" Ch'un-Hua replied, "The shrine to Kuan-yin was built by my master's ancestors. I shall raise some money to have it repaired. Then I shall live there for the rest of my life. I have lost all interest in material goods and wealth."

The villagers helped her collect a sum of money, and after the autumn harvest the farmers brought new thatch and quarried stones to repair the abandoned shrine. And, true to her promise, Ch'un-Hua spent her life tending the shrine. It was said that years later, when Ch'iu Ch'ang-ch'un was meditating in the caves of the Dragon Gate gorge, his spirit communicated with hers and he saw that she had devoted herself to cultivating the Tao. His spirit visited her and gave her instructions to attain enlightenment. Ch'un-Hua practiced diligently, and it was said that she finally attained the Tao and became an immortal.

After Ch'iu Ch'ang-ch'un left Ch'un-Hua, he wandered west and came to a region of the Huang Ho where the river raced through a series of magnificent gorges. The gorge snaked through the mountains like a dragon, and carp could be seen swimming upstream against the raging waters. This gorge was known as the Dragon Gate, and legend said that if a carp succeeded in jumping through the Dragon Gate it would emerge as a dragon. Inspired by the magnificent scenery, Ch'iu Ch'ang-ch'un decided that he would make this his meditation retreat.

Two years passed. One day Ch'iu Ch'ang-ch'un received a vision telling him that a drought was threatening the livelihood of peasants in the nearby villages. The government officials had asked the local priests to pray for rain, but the drought only intensified. Ch'iu Ch'ang-ch'un left his cave and journeyed to the stricken villages. Arriving at the governor's office, he announced that he would pray for rain. The governor was delighted and quickly ordered the guards to build an altar to Ch'iu Ch'ang-ch'un's specifications. When all was ready, Ch'iu Ch'ang-ch'un mounted the platform, prostrated himself on the ground and petitioned the Jade Emperor to grant rain to the region. Before the petition was finished, dark clouds appeared in the sky. The wind rose, and lightning was seen. Soon the rain fell; it continued falling for three days and three nights. The year's crops were saved, and people from the villages talked about an immortal who had the power to command the wind and the rain.

26

The next year there was a drought in the northern plains. Farmlands surrounding the capital city were threatened with the loss of the entire year's crop. The emperor made offerings to the Lords of Heaven and prayed for rain, but the drought only intensified. In despair the emperor called together his ministers and said, "If the rains do not come this season, there will be famine in the capital and many will starve to death. I have done all I could. Is there anyone among you who has an idea as to how we could ask the Lords of Heaven for rain?" One elderly minister replied, "Sire, I have heard that there are people who command tremendous power. They can summon rain and control the elements. Let us ask the governors of each province to locate such persons and present them to us."

The next day an imperial edict was issued to all the governors. The governor of the province where Ch'iu Ch'ang-ch'un had successfully prayed for rain sought out the Taoist monk. When the governor explained to Ch'iu Ch'ang-ch'un what the emperor's edict was about, Ch'iu Ch'ang-ch'un at once consented to accompany the governor to the emperor's palace.

When the emperor saw Ch'iu Ch'ang-ch'un he recognized that the Taoist monk was a man of power. Respectfully he addressed Ch'iu Ch'ang-ch'un: "Taoist master, I am honored to receive you as a guest of the capital. If there is anything you need, please do not hesitate to let my ministers know." Ch'iu Ch'ang-ch'un bowed and replied, "Sire, you are indeed a great ruler, for you place the welfare of your people above everything else. Let us not delay matters. Tomorrow I shall pray for rain. I shall need a platform on which an altar should be placed. I shall petition the Jade Emperor, and within three days the rains will come."

Early the next day Ch'iu Ch'ang-ch'un and the emperor ascended the altar. The emperor offered incense, returned to his seat under the canopy, and waited. Ch'iu Ch'ang-ch'un prostrated himself before the altar, uttered incantations, and prayed for three days under the hot sun. On the third day, at noon, when the sun was high in the sky, a small black cloud appeared. The cloud grew in size until it covered the sky. Strong winds rose and flashes of lightning could be seen. Suddenly, with a clap of thunder, rains poured from the sky and did not stop until the next day. The crops in the surrounding countryside were saved, and the famine was averted.

The emperor was so impressed with Ch'iu Ch'ang-ch'un's powers that he made the Taoist monk his religious adviser. Ch'iu Ch'ang-ch'un was given a residence within the Imperial Palace, and often the emperor would seek out his company for advice on matters of spiritual training. One day the emperor and Ch'iu Ch'ang-ch'un were sitting in a pavilion overlooking a lake filled with lotus blossoms. There was a silence while both men enjoyed the serenity of the quiet lake and lush green garden. Suddenly, the emperor sighed and said, "I wish I could retire from the matters of government so that I could study the teachings of the Tao. But I am afraid this is wishful thinking. I have no son. There is no heir to whom I can pass on my responsibilities." Ch'iu Ch'ang-ch'un smiled and said, "Sire, if I am not mistaken, I think that the empress is pregnant." The emperor could scarcely hide his excitement. "Enlightened master, will it be a boy or girl?" Ch'iu Ch'ang-ch'un replied, "You will have a male child."

That evening, the emperor related his conversation with Ch'iu Ch'ang-ch'un to the empress. The empress said, "The destiny of your empire lies in the birth of our child. Maybe we ought to consult another source as well, just to be sure that the Taoist master's predictions are well founded. I know of a Buddhist monk who possess great powers of divination. He is a Zen Master; his name is Pai-yün. He is the abbot of the White Cloud Monastery." The emperor nodded in agreement and said, "Then let us summon Pai-yün and see what he has to say."

The next day Pai-yün appeared before the emperor. The emperor said to the Buddhist monk, "Zen master, tell me, will the empress give birth to a boy or girl?" Zen Master Pai-yün replied, "According to my divination, the empress will give birth to a girl." The emperor did not like what he heard. He looked at Pai-yün and said, "Master, are you sure? Yesterday the Taoist master Ch'iu Ch'ang-ch'un told me that I shall have an heir."

祈甘霖
天轉日
施妙術
鳳偷龍

子恆

Ch'iu Ch'ang-ch'un prays for rain in the capital city at the request of the emperor.

155

Pai-yün said, "Sire, I am absolutely sure." The emperor then turned to Ch'iu Ch'ang-ch'un and said, "What can you say about this?" Ch'iu Ch'ang-ch'un replied, "It will be a male child." Pai-yün laughed and said to Ch'iu Ch'ang-ch'un, "I think this time you are in error. My divination never fails." Ch'iu Ch'ang-ch'un said, "It may be that the empress originally conceived a female child. But, because the emperor prayed for rain to save his people from famine, the Lords of Heaven may reward his majesty for his virtuous deeds and change the female fetus to a male." Pai-yün said, "I have never heard of such ridiculous things. But if you are so confident that the emperor will have a male child, then let us each place a bet. If the empress gives birth to a boy, I shall give you White Cloud Monastery. However, if the empress gives birth to a girl, then what will you do?" Without hesitation, Ch'iu Ch'ang-ch'un said, "I shall present you with my head." Their wager was written out and signed in the presence of the emperor.

That night Pai-yün divined again. He was uneasy about Ch'iu Ch'ang-ch'un's confidence, and he wanted to be sure that his divinations were accurate. But time after time his oracle told him that the empress was carrying a female child. Satisfied, he said to himself, "Now I shall surely win this bet. Ch'iu Ch'ang-ch'un, don't blame me when you lose your head!"

When Ch'iu Ch'ang-ch'un returned to his quarters that same night, he prepared a talisman and sent it to the palace of the Empress of Heaven. The talisman summoned a powerful fairy who was capable of changing shapes and forms. On the night when the empress was about to give birth, the fairy appeared before Ch'iu Ch'ang-ch'un and said, "Master, you summoned me to help. What do you want me to do?" Ch'iu Ch'ang-ch'un said, "Go to the chamber of the empress. When the baby is born, I want you to open your gourd, capture the spirit of the female baby, and replace it with a male." The fairy bowed and said, "Master, it shall be done."

Late that night the empress gave birth. The midwife who delivered the child sent a message to the emperor: "Your majesty, the nation is blessed by the presence of a princess." The emperor looked at the message for a long time and sighed. "So it was a girl."

The next day, the emperor's court was filled with well-wishers. Zen Master Pai-yün and Ch'iu Ch'ang-ch'un were also present. The emperor ascended his throne and announced in a loud voice, "Last night, the empress gave birth to a princess." At once Pai-yün stepped forward and said, "I have won my bet. Let matters between Ch'iu Ch'ang-ch'un and myself be settled." The emperor did not want Ch'iu Ch'ang-ch'un to lose his life. So he calmly said, "This is a day of celebration. I do not want blood shed on this day. Let me propose that instead of losing his head, Ch'iu Ch'ang-ch'un pay ten thousand pieces of gold for the renovation of White Cloud Monastery. And furthermore, since Ch'iu Ch'ang-ch'un saved my people from famine by calling down rain, I shall reward him with ten thousand pieces of gold." The emperor hoped that if he gave White Cloud Monastery a huge endowment, the abbot Pai-yün would not demand Ch'iu Ch'ang-ch'un's head. But Pai-yün said, "You Majesty, the wager was written out clearly, and you yourself witnessed the signing of the agreement. We cannot undo that which has been sealed." Before the emperor could respond, Ch'iu Ch'ang-ch'un smiled and said, "I have not lost. Let us examine the newborn child together. Maybe the midwife was so excited that she made a mistake in her report." The court officials murmured agreement and said, "Sire, let the child be brought here so that we can all see for ourselves." The emperor was now beginning to have doubts himself. He immediately ordered his personal attendants to fetch the baby.

The child was brought to the emperor, and a hush fell over the crowd as the emperor examined the child. Holding the baby up, the emperor exclaimed, "I have a son!" The nobles and court officials gathered around and looked at the newborn baby. Satisfied that the baby was a boy, they complimented Ch'iu Ch'ang-ch'un on his great powers of divination. Pai-yün could not conceal his puzzlement and agitation. As if he could not believe it, he examined the baby over and over again. He could not understand how he could have made a mistake in his divination. Little did he know that after the baby's birth the fairy had captured the spirit of the female child and replaced it with a male.

The emperor turned to Pai-yün and said, "Mistakes can occur

anytime. You made a mistake in your divination, and the midwife made a mistake in her report. Let this matter between you and Ch'iu Ch'ang-ch'un be settled. You shall prepare to sign the papers that will transfer the ownership of White Cloud Monastery to Ch'iu Ch'ang-ch'un." Pai-yün had nothing to say. Embarrassed, he left the imperial palace and returned to his monastery.

That night Pai-yün paced around the monastery grounds. He was ashamed that he had brought on the transfer of a prosperous monastery to a Taoist monk. His uneasiness was noticed by one of the elders of the monastery, who said, "Abbot, I have a plan. Tomorrow, when Ch'iu Ch'ang-ch'un comes to claim the monastery, we can tell him that unless he finds enough Taoist monks to match the numbers of the Buddhist monks here, he cannot claim the monastery. And we can tell the emperor that without a sufficient number of monks living in the monastery, the grounds will be left unattended. No one would want to see a prosperous monastery fall to neglect and ruin." Pai-yün laughed and said, "Tomorrow let us see that Taoist monk come up with enough people to match the number of monks we have here."

27

Early the next morning Zen Master Pai-yün and his monks sat in the main hall of the monastery and awaited the arrival of Ch'iu Ch'ang-ch'un. When Ch'iu Ch'ang-ch'un appeared, Pai-yün said, "Taoist master, I am afraid that unless you can find enough Taoist monks to match the number of Buddhist monks in this monastery you cannot take charge of these premises honorably. White Cloud Monastery is prosperous and renowned as a center of learning. If there are not sufficient monks to manage the premises then White Cloud Monastery will fall to ruin and neglect. Surely you do not want to see this happen." Ch'iu Ch'ang-ch'un replied, "That is no problem. I have a group of monks waiting for me at the bottom of the hill. Let us exchange monks, one for one."

Ch'iu Ch'ang-ch'un stepped outside the monastery and took his whisk out of his sleeves. Gently he blew at the whisk, and a wind rose. The wind whipped up some dry leaves and carried them down the hill. Returning to the monastery, he said to Pai-yün, "My monks are ready. For every one of your monks who descends the hill, one of my monks will ascend. In this way, we can be sure that the numbers I bring will match your numbers."

How do you think Ch'iu Ch'ang-ch'un managed to produce a large group of Taoist monks on such short notice? The dry leaves that the wind had whipped up and sent down the hill were changed into monks. At the command of Ch'iu Ch'ang-ch'un, they took life for a short time and occupied White Cloud Monastery until the exchange of Buddhist and Taoist monks was completed and Pai-yün and his followers had left.

Why did Ch'iu Ch'ang-ch'un want to gain possession of White Cloud Monastery? Ch'iu Ch'ang-ch'un could not only command the elements but could see into the past and future. He saw that Zen Master Pai-yün had lived a life of comfort in a large and rich monastery. He had become proud and haughty and had forgotten the hardships he had faced during his humble beginnings. If Pai-yün had not been turned out of his monastery to experience such hardships once again, many of the good works that he had accumulated would have become as nothing. Moreover, the Buddhist monks of White Cloud Monastery possessed great learning, but they had been content to live in isolation studying the Buddhist scriptures. Now that they were scattered, they would be forced to set up new temples and monasteries and carry their learning far from the capital city.

As soon as Ch'iu Ch'ang-ch'un took charge of White Cloud Monastery, he sent messages around, announcing that White Cloud Monastery would be accepting novices as well as experienced Taoist monks. Ch'iu Ch'ang-ch'un's reputation had grown tremendously since he had called down rain to save the farmlands. Monks appeared in groups of five and ten, and soon White Cloud Monastery was completely staffed with cooks, gardeners, chanters, and scholars.

As more monks joined the ranks of the White Cloud community, Ch'iu Ch'ang-ch'un felt that he needed to remind his monks of the purpose of living in a Taoist monastery. He assembled all the monks together in the main hall and spoke to them.

"I would like to speak about the meaning of becoming a monk. As you know, monks are people who have left their families and abandoned the 'ways of the world.' When you leave the world, you must leave it with the right attitude. You must become unattached to the world because this is correct and natural to you. Some people become monks because they do not want to deal with the difficulty of everyday life. This is escapism; it is not cultivating the Tao. Again, some become monks because they are poor and becoming a monk gives them the security of not having to worry about where their next meal comes from. This is laziness; it is not cultivating the Tao. Then there are those who come to the monastery because they have lost their families and they seek a place where they can be taken care of. If you enter the monastery with these attitudes, then you will only see the Taoist community as a means of achieving some short-term goals. The goal of attaining the Tao will never be realized."

Ch'iu Ch'ang-ch'un continued. "You have all chosen to become a part of this Taoist community. I accept you and will not

諭吾人
諄諄
告誡
論修行
層層
做來
子桓

*Ch'iu Ch'ang-ch'un and his company of Taoist monks greet
Zen Master Pai-yün.*

turn you away. Whether or not you came with the true intention of cultivating the Tao does not matter. However, if you came with the wrong intention, you should work on correcting it. You have arrived in the Land of the Three Treasures. In some way, your karma has brought you here. There are some among you who are wealthy. You must realize that when you have completed your time here you will possess nothing. There are three ways of entering the Tao. Those who walk the highest path meditate and cultivate the internal energy. Those who walk the middle path chant the scriptures devotedly. Those who walk the lower path do good deeds by attending to the daily chores in the monastery. Perform that which others find it difficult to do. Be able to live with that which others find it difficult to live with. Let your emotions dissolve. Do what you think is impossible. In this way your mind will be empty, and the monsters of illusion will not be able to capture you. If your mind is emptied of thoughts, then how can the ego exist? Let there be no duality between you and others: no ego of your own and in your mind no egos of others.

"You must seek the Tao naturally. Do not force yourself. Do what you can do. Do not attempt what is beyond you at the moment. Some are destined to walk the highest path, others the middle, and yet others the lower path. Accept your path and walk it diligently. Those who walk the lower paths should not envy the ones who walk the higher path. For if you attempt to obtain what is not yours, then you will lose the fruits that were meant for you. Not everybody will become an immortal in his or her lifetime. The important thing is that you do your part in this lifetime. Even if you do not attain immortality, you will have been a good person.

"The shaved head of a Buddhist and the topknot of a Taoist do not make a monk. If your mind is still attached to forms, if you have not dissolved the attachments to "I" and "Other," "past" and "future," then even though you may don the attire of a monk your heart will still be like that of a wild animal. If you still harbor greed, envy, desire for fame and riches, you are not truly one who has abandoned the world. Many who don the attire of the monk delight in the security of their life-style. They think they have found a comfortable life. If you possess these attitudes, then it would be better that you return to the world, for you will accumulate bad karma in the end."

While Ch'iu Ch'ang-ch'un was speaking to his monks, a crowd of men gathered in front of the monastery. These men were tall and strong and appeared to be skilled in the arts of fighting. They were led by a man who seemed to command respect from the rest of the group, for as they reached the monastery gate, the leader motioned the men to stop and check their attire before entering. "We must appear respectful before the teacher," he said. This man was none other than Chao Pi, the bandit chief of T'ai Shan, who had fed Ch'iu Ch'ang-ch'un and prevented him from starving to death. After parting with Ch'iu Ch'ang-ch'un, Chao Pi and his followers had given up living outside the law. With the money they had accumulated during their bandit days they settled in the towns and villages and made an honest living as merchants or farmers. Ten years had passed, and one day Chao Pi heard that a Taoist monk by the name of Ch'iu Ch'ang-ch'un was inviting seekers of the Tao to White Cloud Monastery. Chao Pi assembled his friends and said to them, "Remember how ten years ago on T'ai Shan we met a starving Taoist monk? Thanks to his advice, we are now living upright and honest lives. I have heard that this Taoist master is now in charge of a large monastery in the capital and is inviting people who are interested in Taoist training to live there. All these years I have been waiting for a chance to become a Taoist monk. I believe my chance has come. I plan to go to White Cloud Monastery and ask Master Ch'iu Ch'ang oh'un to be my teacher. If the rest of you are interested, let us make the journey together." The men nodded and said, "Brother, we have been waiting for that chance as well. Let us go immediately. We have no more attachments to this world."

As Chao Pi and his friends entered the main hall of the monastery, they met a Taoist monk who greeted them amicably, "Well met, my friends. How have you been since we parted?" Chao Pi and his friends were dumbfounded. They scratched their chins and murmured to themselves, "Who is this monk? We have never met him before. How come he acts as if he knows us?" Aloud, Chao Pi stammered, "Taoist master, excuse me, I have forgotten. Have we met before? We came to ask Master

Ch'iu Ch'ang-ch'un to receive us as disciples. Could you please lead us to him?" The Taoist monk replied, "I am Ch'iu Ch'ang-ch'un. Ten years ago on T'ai Shan you saved me from starvation." Chao Pi and his friends fell on their knees and said, "Master, forgive us for not recognizing you. We expected you to be much older but you look younger than when we parted ten years ago. We, on the other hand, have grown old." Another man spoke up, "Master, we heard that you were inviting seekers of the Tao to White Cloud Monastery. We would like to become your disciples and live as monks in the monastery. Sir, please accept us as your students."

Ch'iu Ch'ang-ch'un said to them, "I am grateful to you all for saving my life at T'ai Shan. And I know that since we parted you have lived upright and honest lives. Now that you have seen through the illusions of the material world and have decided to become monks, it is an occasion to be celebrated. But to become a monk is no simple matter. You have come this far because in your past lives you accumulated some good works, and in your present lives you have been able to correct your wrongdoings. From now on, you are members of a Taoist community. You must obey the rules of discipline of the monastery. You must develop a heart of compassion and tame your wild temper. Do not let your bad temper disrupt the serenity of the monastic grounds. Respect all sentient beings. Have pity on those whose intelligence and intuition are lower than yours. Their progress is slow because their time has not yet come. Do not be jealous of those who are more advanced than you in their training. Their progress is rapid because their foundations are strong. The Tao is indiscriminate to rich and poor. To those who value virtue and learning, the Tao is like a precious jewel. To those others who see no value in virtue and learning, the Tao is like dry twigs. Lay down your attachment to riches. For in the Tao, uprightness and sacrifice are more valuable than wealth. Thus it is said that in the Tao there is no difference between a king and a pauper."

Ch'iu Ch'ang-ch'un continued. "When I was young I realized that I had no desire for living in the material world. So I journeyed far to seek out a Taoist master for whom I could learn from. My teacher, Wang Ch'ung-yang, instructed me in the teachings of the Tao. My brother Ma Tan-yang helped me when I lost hope. I have suffered many hardships throughout my life. I have been starved seventy-two times. Each time I almost lost my life. But I did not give up. I continued to temper my heart and worked hard to overcome the obstacles in my way. For six years, in rain or shine, I carried people across a river. Eventually I came to the attention of the emperor because I prayed to the Lords of Heaven to relieve a drought in a remote province. I have not attained the Tao but even to make small steps along the way required perseverance and discipline. If you take the oath of a monk, you must be prepared to face whatever hardships that will confront you in your attempts to cultivate the Tao. Overcome ten obstacles, and you will have banished ten monsters from your mind. Overcome a hundred obstacles, and you will have banished one hundred monsters from your mind."

Chao Pi and his friends bowed again and said, "May we be worthy of the master's teachings." Ch'iu Ch'ang-ch'un welcomed them into the monastery, and on an auspicious day Chao Pi and his friends took the monk's oath and became disciples of Ch'iu Ch'ang-ch'un.

Since the birth of his heir, the emperor had been convinced that Ch'iu Ch'ang-ch'un was an immortal. Each day as soon as he had taken care of his administrative affairs he would seek out Ch'iu Ch'ang-ch'un for spiritual advice. Often, the emperor would stay up late into the night discussing the Taoist scriptures with Ch'iu Ch'ang-ch'un. The empress, however, was very unhappy. She could not stop thinking to herself, "I know for certain that I gave birth to a girl. How could the sex of the baby have changed when it was brought before the emperor? Moreover, this incident caused my teacher Pai-yün to lose his monastery. I must get to the bottom of this matter."

One evening, while the emperor was with Ch'iu Ch'ang-ch'un, the empress sent for Pai-yün. When Pai-yün arrived at the empress's residence, he said, "Lady, I see that you are unhappy. What is bothering you?" The empress replied, "Master, I have been feeling guilty ever since you lost the monastery to that Taoist monk. I feel that my child is the cause of all the problems. I just don't understand how my baby could have changed from a girl to a boy." Pai-yün said, "I am sure that Ch'iu Ch'ang-ch'un is at the bottom of this. He must have commanded an evil spirit to steal the soul of your girl and exchange it for a boy. I fear some evil force is at work. You should warn the emperor at once." The empress sighed and said, "The emperor will never listen to me. In his eyes Ch'iu Ch'ang-ch'un is an immortal. And besides, he wanted an heir. If I were to tell him that the son we have is the work of an evil force, I am afraid that I would be charged with treason." Pai-yün said, "I have a plan. Do you know the bit of history in the T'ang dynasty in which the T'ang emperor administered a test to find out whether the Taoist master Chang Kuo-lao was an immortal? Chang Kuo-lao was believed to be an immortal by many of the court officials and nobility. The T'ang emperor did not believe it, and to test the Taoist master's credibility he prepared a strong poison and mixed it with an aromatic wine. Chang Kuo-lao was invited to the imperial palace. In the presence of the nobility and the court officials, the emperor offered Chang Kuo-lao the poisoned wine. Chang Kuo-lao drank three cupfuls and exclaimed, "What good wine!" A few seconds later he keeled over with his mouth open. His teeth turned black, and he lay there for half an hour. Everybody thought that Chang Kuo-lao was dead. But then he rose, spit out the blackened teeth, and closed his mouth. When he opened his mouth again, new white teeth had grown in. The T'ang emperor finally believed that Chang Kuo-lao was an immortal." Pai-yün paused and continued. "Your Highness, you could administer the same test to Ch'iu Ch'ang-ch'un. Invite him for dinner and serve him poisoned wine. If he is truly an immortal, then the poison should not affect him. If he is a fraud, then we would rid ourselves of this evil monk." The empress nodded and said, "That is a good idea." A messenger was sent to White Cloud Monastery to invite Ch'iu Ch'ang-ch'un to the empress's residence for dinner the next evening.

28

When an imperial emissary arrived at White Cloud Monastery to present the empress's invitation to Ch'iu Ch'ang-ch'un, Ch'iu Ch'ang-ch'un already knew of the empress's intentions. He accepted the invitation and then instructed his disciples to fill twenty-four tubs with cold water. "Make sure you have them ready. I shall need them when I return. My life and death depend on them." Ch'iu Ch'ang-ch'un then went to the imperial palace.

When the empress saw Ch'iu Ch'ang-ch'un she said, "Taoist Master, your powers of divination are indeed impressive. You predicted that I would give birth to a boy, and the country now has a crown prince. Let me express my gratitude and admiration by offering you three cups of wine. The wine is specially prepared and is reserved for the emperor and myself." The empress then ordered her attendant to present a large cup of wine to Ch'iu Ch'ang-ch'un. He took the cup and emptied in one mouthful. Two more cups were filled, and Ch'iu Ch'ang-ch'un drank again.

After his audience with the empress, Ch'iu Ch'ang-ch'un returned to the monastery and immediately jumped into the first tub of cold water. When the water became hot, he got out and jumped into the next tub. When Ch'iu Ch'ang-ch'un got into the twenty-forth tub, he found that the water came up only to his chest. The disciples had not filled the tub to the brim. Because he was only half submerged in the cold water, the poison that remained in the upper part of his body could not be neutralized. It rose to the top of his head and burned off some of his hair, leaving a bald spot on the top of his head.

When the empress heard that Ch'iu Ch'ang-ch'un had not died from drinking the poisoned wine, she summoned Zen Master Pai-yün and said to him, "Now I have no doubts that Ch'iu Ch'ang-ch'un is an immortal. He did not die from drinking my poisoned wine." Pai-yün replied, "Your Majesty, it might be that the poison was not strong enough. I have a better plan to determine whether Ch'iu Ch'ang-ch'un is a fraud or not. It is said that Taoist immortals can change the shape of metals, especially gold and silver. They can make a lump of gold square or round or flat. We can present Ch'iu Ch'ang-ch'un with a bar of gold and ask him to wear it around his head. If he can flatten the piece of gold into a headband, then he is an immortal. If not, he will feel so embarrassed that he will go into hiding and never return to the capital city."

Again the empress invited Ch'iu Ch'ang-ch'un to the palace. When Ch'iu Ch'ang-ch'un appeared before the empress, she saw that he had a large bald spot at the center of his head. When asked what had happened to his hair, Ch'iu Ch'ang-ch'un calmly replied, "Last night the empress presented me with the wine of immortality. It was so strong that the Gate of Heaven on top of my head was opened, enabling my spirit to ascend to the Palace of the Immortals." The empress was ashamed because she knew what Ch'iu Ch'ang-ch'un was referring to. Still, she had promised Zen Master Pai-yün to test Ch'iu Ch'ang-ch'un one more time. Thus she said, "Taoist Master, you are indeed an immortal. Receive a gold headband from me. When you wear it, people will know that you are the spiritual teacher of the emperor and empress." An attendant brought Ch'iu Ch'ang-ch'un a gold bar. Ch'iu Ch'ang-ch'un took the gold bar and gently blew at it. When the fires of his internal energy fanned the gold, the bar became as soft as mud. Ch'iu Ch'ang-ch'un took the softened gold, fashioned it into a headband, and tied it around his head. It is said that from then on Taoist monks have worn yellow headbands on festive occasions.

The empress was both shocked and ashamed. She stood up and said apologetically, "Master, it was my fault that I doubted your credibility. I hope you will forgive my ignorance and folly." Ch'iu Ch'ang-ch'un bowed and replied, "Your majesty, the fault is not yours. There are obstacles that I need to surmount before I can complete my training." When Pai-yün heard these words he came into the room. Bowing to Ch'iu Ch'ang-ch'un, he said, "Master, the fault is all mine. The monsters of illusion have captured my thoughts. It was I who directed the empress to test you." Ch'iu Ch'ang-ch'un said, "It was I who started this course

賜鴆酒皇后試戴道冠真金人吟詩
子祖

The empress presents poisoned wine to Ch'iu Ch'ang-ch'un.

169

of events. Master, you have reached the stage of total emptiness. How can the monsters enter your mind?" Pai-yün thought to himself, "I have tried to harm him. Yet he does not harbor any grudge." Aloud he said, "Let the past be the past. Winning or losing no longer matters."

The empress was delighted that Ch'iu Ch'ang-ch'un and Pai-yün had come to a peaceful reconciliation. She ordered her attendants to bring wine to celebrate the occasion. Then the door guards announced that the emperor had arrived. Seeing the empress and the two monks celebrating, the emperor said, "Messangers told me that the two masters have resolved their differences. I was so excited that I came over here immediately so that I could be part of this happy occasion." The empress then described the course of events to the emperor, and the emperor said, "Now that Master Ch'iu Ch'ang-ch'un and Master Pai-yün are friends I cannot be happier. I have always felt that Buddhism, Confucianism, and Taoism follow similar principles." He then turned to Ch'iu Ch'ang-ch'un and Pai-yün and said, "I shall decree that a new Buddhist monastery be erected in the capital city. When the construction is completed, the Buddhist icons and relics from White Cloud Monastery shall be moved to their new home. A new statue of Lao-tzu will be erected at White Cloud Monastery to honor the founding patriarch of Taoism. In this way, both Taoists and Buddhists will have a temple in the capital city. May the fragrance of their incense never vanish in the thousands of years to come." Pai-yün and Ch'iu Ch'ang-ch'un bowed low and thanked the emperor.

Although Pai-yün had resolved his conflict with Ch'iu Ch'ang-ch'un, some Buddhist monks still bore a grudge toward the Taoists who occupied White Cloud Monastery. This faction was led by a hot-tempered young monk who had gathered a small following around him. He summoned his followers together and said to them, "Ch'iu Ch'ang-ch'un and the Taoists think that they can occupy White Cloud Monastery forever. Let us make things difficult for them. I propose that we build a Buddhist monastery behind White Cloud Monastery. Our monastery will be named West Wind Monastery. As the saying goes, 'The west wind blows away the white clouds,' I predict that once our

monastery is built Ch'iu Ch'ang-ch'un and his Taoists will encounter bad luck, and White Cloud Monastery wil fall to ruin."
The monks cheered. The plan was outlined on paper and
presented to Pai-yün. When Pai-yün saw the proposal he said,
"Whose idea is this? And why are you proposing this?" An elderly
monk stepped forward and said, "It was the idea of this young
bodhisattva." The hotheaded young monk stood up before Zen
Master Pai-yün. Pai-yün questioned him. "Why do you want to
build the West Wind Monastery behind the White Cloud Monastery?" The young monk replied, "Master, they took our property. I wish to avenge the shame and discomfort that have been
brought upon us." Pai-yün said, "In Buddhism there is no place
for revenge. In our heart is only emptiness. If you harbour
thoughts of shame, vengeance, and discomfort, your heart is not
clear of the specks of dust from the material world. When the
Buddha was tortured by the barbarian king and his flesh was cut
from his body, the Lord Buddha did not harbor any thoughts of
revenge. In any case, Ch'iu Ch'ang-ch'un and the Taoists did not
occupy White Cloud Monastery unfairly. The wager was docu-
mented before the emperor. I lost the wager and therefore
forfeited the monastery. The Taoists did not take the monastery
by force. The other day the emperor announced that a Buddhist
monastery will be built for us. If you cause trouble with your
ideas, the emperor may withdraw his favor. Moreover, your plans
amount to ridiculing the emperor's wishes. I shall not support
your plan. If you want to build a West Wind Monastery, you are
on your own. I do not want any part in it."

The monks sat in silence for a long time. They began to
understand Pai-yün's rationale and one by one, the thoughts of
the "west wind blowing away the white cloud" dissolved, except
in the mind of the hotheaded young monk. He left Pai-yün and
the other monks and said to himself, "That bunch of fools! I
don't need their help. I shall raise the money myself." So the
monk began to approach the wealthy families of the capital,
saying that the Buddhists needed to show that they were stronger
than the Taoists and that the West Wind Monastery would drive
the White Cloud Taoist Monastery to ruin. Few listened to the
wild claims of the monk, but when some of the Taoist monks of

White Cloud Monastery heard about West Wind Monastery they laughed among themselves and said, "If the West Wind Monastery is situated behind us, all we need to do is to build a large wall so that the west wind will get bounced right back into their monastery!" The joking went on and someone said, "When the wind returns to West Wind Monastery, let's have it carry a little flame with it. With a little magic, West Wind Monastery will surely burn down."

Gossip ran wild in the capital. What had been intended as a joke became history. And over the years, children would retell the story of how in a duel of Buddhist and Taoist magic, West Wind Monastery (which in fact never existed) was burned down.

29

After his reconciliation with Zen Master Pai-yün, Ch'iu Ch'ang-ch'un left the daily administrative matters of White Cloud Monastery to his senior disciples and withdrew into solitude in preparation for his departure from the mortal realm. Drawing from his experience of the obstacles that he had encountered during his training, Ch'iu Ch'ang-ch'un wrote a book called *Journey to the West.* In it he discussed the pitfalls that obstruct the path to enlightenment. He described the emotions and desires that the seeker of the Tao would have to overcome. He likened the monsters of the mind to wild horses. He warned of laziness and greed, and he described uncultivated intelligence as a mischievous monkey. After the book was completed Ch'iu Ch'ang-ch'un sought out his friend Pai-yün and presented it to him. Pai-yün was an enlightened person, and when he read Ch'iu Ch'ang-ch'un's book he recognized immediately that Ch'iu Ch'ang-ch'un was describing the internal changes that occur in the mind and body as the internal alchemical work progresses. Inspired by Ch'iu Ch'ang-ch'un's work, Pai-yün also wrote a book documenting the experiences and visions that occur on the path to enlightenment. The book was titled *Legends of the Gods.* Together, these two books offer guidance to those who seek enlightenment.

It is said that Ch'iu Ch'ang-ch'un attained enlightenment shortly afterward and ascended to the Palace of Heaven. He was received by many immortals and heavenly lords. When he arrived before the Jade Emperor, Immortal Lü, and the Lords of Heaven, Earth, and Water, he saw the other six disciples of Wang Ch'ung-yang. They had all attained the Tao and were waiting for the Empress of Heaven and the Jade Emperor to confer upon them the status of immortality.

The Lords of Heaven, Earth, and Water unfolded a scroll and read aloud the accomplishments of each of the seven disciples. Ch'iu Ch'ang-ch'un was first on the list. He was commended for his unshakable faith and endurance in his training and pursuit of the Tao. Second on the list was Liu Ch'ang-sheng; he was commended for his intuitive understanding of the mysterious ways of the Tao. Third was T'an Ch'ang-chen, who was commended for his stability in attitude and behavior. Fourth on the list was Ma Tan-yang. He was commended for his quiet and calm disposition and his simple and straightforward approach to the Tao. Fifth on the list was Hao T'ai-ku. Throughout his training his attitude was untainted by material and personal interest. Sixth was Wang Yü-yang, who was commended for his steadfastness in maintaining stillness in the midst of confusion and conflict. After the six names were mentioned, the Lords of Heaven, Earth, and Water continued, "Sun-Pu-erh was the first to embrace the Tao. In accomplishment, she far surpassed the rest. It was due to her intelligence and wisdom that the rest of the group was initiated into the Tao. So as she led the initiation into the Tao, she will complete the attainment of the Tao. She will be placed seventh, for the last place is reserved for the one who achieves the highest enlightenment."

After the accomplishments of the Seven Taoist Masters were read before an audience of heavenly lords and immortals, the Jade Emperor motioned the seven to step before him to receive the status of immortality. Ma Tang-yang, T'an Ch'ang-chen, Liu Ch'ang-sheng, Sun Pu-erh, Hao T'ai-ku, and Wang Yü-yang all stepped forward and knelt before the Jade Emperor. Only Ch'iu Ch'ang-ch'un stood quietly on the side. Seeing Ch'iu Ch'ang-ch'un's refusal to acknowledge the gift of the Jade Emperor, the Lord of Heaven said in a commanding voice, "Ch'iu Ch'ang-ch'un, why are you disrespectful of the Emperor's gift?" Ch'iu Ch'ang-ch'un prostrated himself before the Jade Emperor and said, "It is not that I am disrespectful, but I feel that the gift offered to me should be given to all those who seek the Tao. My path to enlightenment was fraught with hardships and obstacles. The hardships would turn away many who cannot bear the sufferings that I experienced. I would like to lighten the burden of those who seek the Tao but do not have the disposition to bear the suffering of cold, hunger, and humiliation. Therefore I ask the Emperor to reconsider giving me the gift of immortality so that it might be used to help more people attain the Tao in one lifetime."

受丹詔七真成正果
赴瑤池群仙慶蟠桃

The Empress of Heaven receives the Seven Taoist Masters.

175

There was a long silence. Then suddenly a gust of wind rose and a figure with a red face and red beard materialized in the center of the heavenly gathering. This figure was the Lord of Thunder. Slayer of monsters and guardian of the Taoist principles, he was responsible for issuing rewards and punishments to mortals. The Lord of Thunder bowed before the Jade Emperor and, turning to the heavenly audience, said, "Ch'iu Ch'ang-ch'un need not worry about the welfare of those who seek the Tao. I shall pledge to be the guardian of all who walk the path to enlightenment. My help will be given according to the effort of the seeker. Those who only spend a little effort will receive less help. Those who labor hard in their quest can count on my support without fail. I shall see to it that those who have good intentions do not suffer hunger and cold." When Ch'iu Ch'ang-ch'un heard the words of the Lord of Thunder, he finally bowed before the Jade Emperor to receive the status of immortality.

After their audience with the Jade Emperor, the Seven Taoist Masters were led to other chambers of the Palace of Heaven and introduced to the various gods and immortals residing in the heavenly realm. Then came the day when the immortal peach ripened and all the gods and immortals were invited by the Empress of Heaven to share in the tasting of the peach. As the guests stood before the canopy of the Empress, the Empress addressed them: "Only those who have completed their cultivation of the Tao can taste the peach. One bite of the peach will extend your life one thousand years. May mortals learn well from the examples of the Seven Taoist Masters so that they may also one day taste the peach of immortality!"